# CHILD OF GRACE

### a mother's life changed by a daughter's special needs

## NANCY DOYLE CHALFANT

Harold Shaw Publishers
Wheaton, Illinois

*To Henry*
*and*
*Anne, Henry, Verlinda, and Nancy*
*"If one member suffers, all suffer together; if one member is honored, all rejoice together."*

1 CORINTHIANS 12:16

Scripture quotations are taken from the *Revised Standard Version* of the Bible, copyrighted 1946 and 1952 by the Division of Christian Education of the National Council of Churches, U.S.A and are used by permission.

Copyright © 1988 by Nancy Doyle Chalfant

All rights reserved. No part of this book may be reproduced or transmitted in any form or by any means, electronic or mechanical, including photocopying, recording, or any information storage and retrieval system without written permission from Harold Shaw Publishers, Box 567, Wheaton, Illinois 60189. Printed in the United States of America.

Cover art compliments of the Chalfant family

Edited by Dave and Neta Jackson

ISBN 0-87788-152-9

**Library of Congress Cataloging-in-Publication Data**
Chalfant, Nancy Doyle.
  Child of grace.

  1. Chalfant, Nancy Doyle.  2. Chalfant, Verlinda, 1946-1973.  3. Christian biography—United States. 4. Parents of handicapped children—United States— Biography.  5. Handicapped children—Care—Moral and ethical aspects.  I. Title.
BR1725.C42A3  1988    248.8'6'0924  [B]     88-6462
ISBN 0-87788-152-9

| 97 | 96 | 95 | 94 | 93 | 92 | 91 | 90 | 89 | 88 |
|----|----|----|----|----|----|----|----|----|----|
| 10 | 9  | 8  | 7  | 6  | 5  | 4  | 3  | 2  | 1  |

# Contents

Acknowledgments . . . . . . . . . . . . . . . . . . . . . . . . . . . . . . *vii*
Preface . . . . . . . . . . . . . . . . . . . . . . . . . . . . . . . . . . . . . . . . . *ix*

1  The Miracle Baby . . . . . . . . . . . . . . . . . . . . . . . . . . . . . *1*
2  Descent into Darkness . . . . . . . . . . . . . . . . . . . . . . . . . *7*
3  What Will People Think? . . . . . . . . . . . . . . . . . . . . . . *11*
4  Trapped . . . . . . . . . . . . . . . . . . . . . . . . . . . . . . . . . . . . *17*
5  Loneliness . . . . . . . . . . . . . . . . . . . . . . . . . . . . . . . . . . *21*
6  The Turning Point . . . . . . . . . . . . . . . . . . . . . . . . . . . *27*
7  The Power of Prayer . . . . . . . . . . . . . . . . . . . . . . . . . *33*
8  All Things Are Possible . . . . . . . . . . . . . . . . . . . . . . . *39*
9  Light in the Darkness . . . . . . . . . . . . . . . . . . . . . . . . *47*
10 The Door . . . . . . . . . . . . . . . . . . . . . . . . . . . . . . . . . . *57*
11 Two Strands . . . . . . . . . . . . . . . . . . . . . . . . . . . . . . . *63*
12 A Day in the Life of Verlinda . . . . . . . . . . . . . . . . . . *73*
13 Unseen Things . . . . . . . . . . . . . . . . . . . . . . . . . . . . . *83*
14 Was It Worth It? . . . . . . . . . . . . . . . . . . . . . . . . . . . . *87*
13 Developing Talents . . . . . . . . . . . . . . . . . . . . . . . . . . *93*
16 Pass It Along . . . . . . . . . . . . . . . . . . . . . . . . . . . . . . *101*
17 Is Suffering God's Will? . . . . . . . . . . . . . . . . . . . . . *109*
18 Wholeness At Last . . . . . . . . . . . . . . . . . . . . . . . . . *115*
19 A Life Fulfilled . . . . . . . . . . . . . . . . . . . . . . . . . . . . *123*
20 Verland . . . . . . . . . . . . . . . . . . . . . . . . . . . . . . . . . . *127*
21 Answered Prayer . . . . . . . . . . . . . . . . . . . . . . . . . . *135*

Epilogue . . . . . . . . . . . . . . . . . . . . . . . . . . . . . . . . . . . . . *141*
Appendix: How the Church Can Help . . . . . . . . . . . . . . *145*

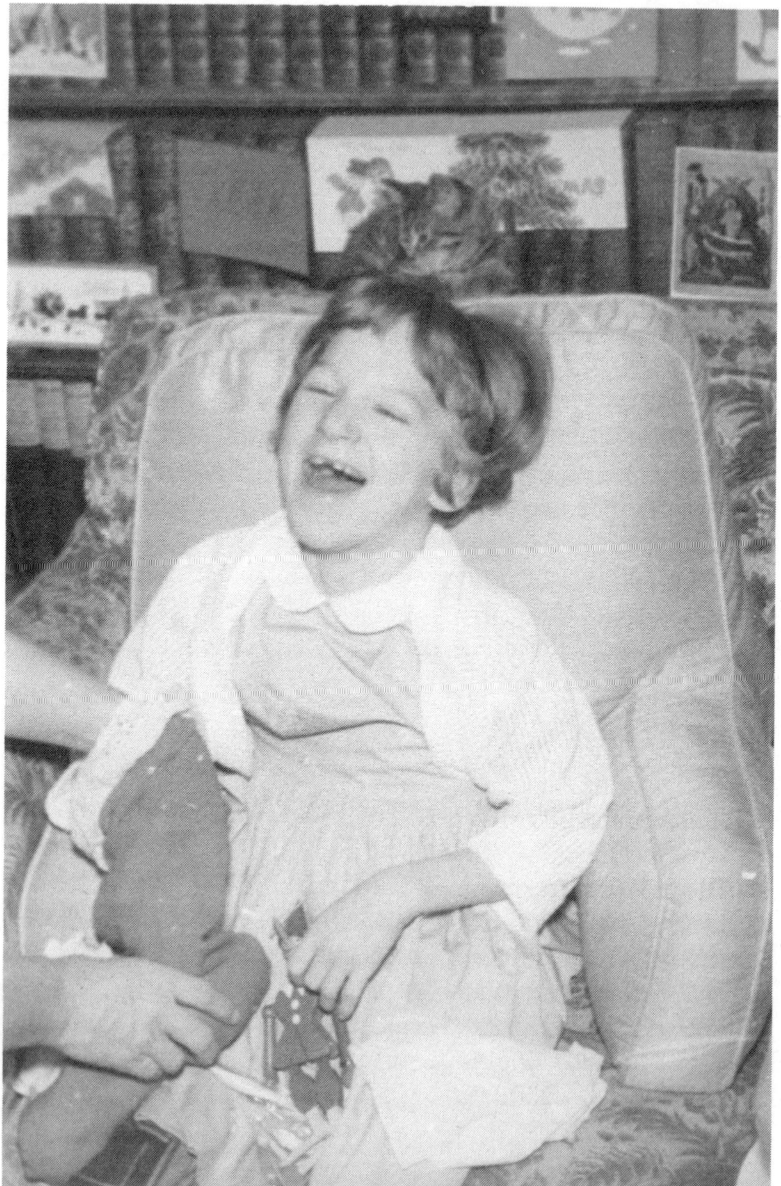

## Acknowledgments

There were many people who participated in bringing this book into a publishable state. First of all my husband, Henry, who shared in it from the beginning and who gave encouragement and wise counsel as the story began to unfold.

I am very grateful for my friend, Betty Mohler, whose excitement over my 1950's writings encouraged me to "do something about them," and who continued being an encourager throughout the years.

I am thankful that Ann Alexander Gordon, a friend with an editing and writing background, appeared on the scene at just the right time to make suggestions and to put in many hours of editing.

My children and their spouses, Anne and Brad Brown, Henry and Kathy Chalfant, and Nano and Jon Chalfant-Walker, deserve special thanks for taking me seriously enough to give me a word processor for Christmas in 1981 when I made my commitment to write this book. Although I mastered their machine for basic operation, I could never have proceeded along at a reasonable pace without the faithful and expert assistance of Liz Shaw, another friend who gave up one day of her week for more than a year to come to my home and transpose my writings to disk form.

Special thanks, too, to Helen Jean Elliott, Administrative Assistant to John Guest, who made sure the manuscript was printed out properly.

David Lied was instrumental in submitting the manuscript to Harold Shaw Publishers by way of Stephen Board. I am grateful for the interest of both, and for Stephen's suggestion that preliminary editing be done by Dave and Neta Jackson, who, by streamlining my original manuscript, deserve my gratitude, as well as the readers'!

Final editing was done by Ramona Cramer Tucker and Annette Heinrich. I am very grateful for their sensitivity and response to the story.

Finally, to John Guest, pastor and friend, to the family of St. Stephen's Church, to Reid Carpenter and the members of the Pittsburgh Offensive, and to all the others who have prayed that this book would find a publisher, I say "thank you!"

## Preface

This morning I feel as though someone has called my bluff: no more talking about writing a book about being the mother of a profoundly retarded child. Now is the day to begin.

I have made a commitment to myself, to others, and to God. It feels impossible, but I know that with God, all things are possible. So I have set my face to tell the story of what happened when Verlinda's life touched mine and how God came to us both from that time on.

Why write either story after all these years? Verlinda was born in 1946, and she died in 1973. Isn't it over and done with? Hasn't the impact she had on my life faded in relevance now? No! Her story is timeless.

Every day someone somewhere is experiencing as devastating a life shock as I experienced the day Verlinda's condition was declared hopeless.

Every day a mother grieves over the news that her child is retarded or disabled.

Every day families fear what the future holds for them as they attempt to find answers to the problem of severe disabilities in a family member.

It is my hope that my experience will bring inspiration, courage, and hope to those who are at the beginning of this long and difficult road.

I began to tell this story in the 1950's. I had received a beautiful gift of faith and was living each day trusting in the promises of God. I wanted to share my knowledge of his love and mercy with all parents.

I was confident that as more of us learned to believe that God's ultimate will was for wholeness, our faith would move mountains, and we would begin to see the retarded made whole.

I still believe that is possible, but a book of advice to parents on the way to handle their situation is an impossibility. Each situation is unique, and no two can be handled exactly alike.

One piece of advice I can offer is to heed the command of Jesus: "Follow me." What a difference those two words can make in our lives! To follow him we need to know something about him. This learning about Jesus, who he is and what he came to do for us, helps us discover that we never need to carry our burden alone. We learn to "abide in him," that his promise, "Lo, I am with you always," is forever true.

Children whose brain cells have been severely impaired are not going to fit into the normal scheme of family life. They are different; how different depends on how severely the brain was damaged. In our daughter, Verlinda, it was very severe, so I am privileged to be familiar with the "least" of God's children.

The birth of a "different" child calls us to make many unfamiliar decisions. Advice pours in from family members, friends, ministers,

*Preface*

and doctors. It is usually given lovingly, with the desire to help. But these people are often as uninformed as we are. Even doctors tend to give advice we are not ready for: "Put your child in an institution," and sometimes, "Forget you ever had him." How do we know whose advice to follow?

The answer is, we don't. We want the best thing for our child; we want the best for the rest of the family. Now is when we learn the value of the command to follow Jesus.

The most important decision our family faced was, should we keep Verlinda at home with us, or would it be better for the other children if we placed her in an institution for the retarded?

Her father and I visited one such institution, a private facility about 300 miles from Sewickley. It was quite a lovely area, a homelike place surrounded by large trees and lawns. However, they had nothing at all for profoundly retarded children. They could offer only the hospital wing for Verlinda. This was certainly not what we wanted for her.

We had an opportunity to meet a psychologist from England, Dr. Alice Buck, a Christian woman who came to help us make this difficult decision. We told her of our concern for Verlinda's sister and brother. We discussed the effect upon them of having Verlinda live at home. Would it curtail the freedom they needed to bring friends home without fear of embarrassment? Would it be such an abnormal life for everyone that it would be damaging to them?

Dr. Buck believed that children usually did not share the same fears the parents felt. She told us that removing Verlinda from the family circle might rather give them a sense of insecurity—that if an illness or accident happened to them, they too would be taken away.

Through our discussion and prayers we came to see that it was best for our family to have Verlinda live at home.

Verlinda was nearly two years old before I came to know Jesus Christ and realized that we couldn't make any "right" decisions on our own. I discovered that prayer and trust in him made the difference and provided the assurance that we were on the right track. Then I was comforted by the words: "Trust in the Lord with all your heart, and lean not on your own understanding. In all your ways acknowledge him, and he shall direct your paths" (Proverbs 3:5-6, NKJV).

We do not know what paths the Lord will lead us down, and we come to understanding and acceptance only by asking, seeking, and knocking as Jesus instructed. God's plan for my life was to be involved in helping to bring about societal changes for the profoundly retarded and the severely handicapped.

Had Verlinda been healed at an early age, God would have had another plan for my life and for hers, too. But Verlinda came into the world when there was nothing for children with severe brain damage. In those days, parents had but two choices.

One was to take care of their child at home, keeping him or her hidden from the community, doing the best they could to give loving, custodial, full-time care within the family circle.

The alternative was to place the child in the large institution where only the higher functioning retarded people without severe physical handicaps received training or had a life beyond the crib. This has been termed "warehousing," a descriptive term for what became of the children who entered those institutions 40 years ago. Verlinda was described as a "crib case," a term still in use, just as is the unfortunate term, "vegetable."

Attitudes have changed, but there is still a long way to go. Until all people everywhere are educated to the point where they refuse to speak of children of the living God, made in His image, as "vegetables," those of us who know better must continue to fight for all people, no matter how incapacitated, to be treated with dignity and respect.

Jesus said, "Let the children come to me, and do not hinder them; for to such belongs the kingdom of heaven" (Matthew 19:14).

Nancy Doyle Chalfant

# 1

# The Miracle Baby

*A time to weep,
and a time to laugh.*
ECCLESIASTES 3:4

When my husband, Henry, came home from World War II, it was exciting to think about adding to our family of two children. Anne was nine and Henry, Jr., five.

But as the months went by, our prospects grew dim. I became depressed and worried because I had had two miscarriages in the past. If I did become pregnant, I would have to be careful.

At last the doctor confirmed that I could expect our third child in the middle of January, 1947. We were thrilled!

Because of my history I wasn't surprised when the doctor informed me that I must spend a large part of my time in bed during the first few months. I was also told that I should have a new blood test to determine whether my blood was Rh-negative or Rh-positive. Apparently if a mother's blood is negative and the father's positive, complications can result for the baby. We were relieved to learn that my blood was Rh-positive.

As the months passed, I was up and about, and everything seemed normal. In mid-December Henry received an "okay" to go off for a weekend of duck shooting in Maryland with his brother-in-law and some friends. And it was that weekend when our eagerly anticipated baby came into the world, the seventeenth of December, 1946. She weighed six and a half pounds, a good size for a "preemie," and I was proud that I had produced another healthy baby.

Henry hurried home, and we rejoiced together over our new little girl. The other children had been named for Henry's side of the family, so we decided that this baby would be named for someone on my side of the family. We chose Verlinda after my father's mother as a special name for a special and much wanted baby.

The first time I saw Verlinda, I was amazed at her hands. Her fingers were long and slender, and I saw that she had interlaced them, one hand with the other. I did not know that newborn babies had such a skill, and it triggered my imagination. I dreamed that she would be musically gifted and those long slender fingers would fly over the piano keys.

I felt content and fulfilled as a person during the two days after Verlinda's birth. Having three children made us more of a family and erased the three years of separation caused by the war and Henry's overseas duty. We would begin again and watch another new life develop.

Suddenly those contented dreams were shattered! Verlinda became desperately ill, turning orange with jaundice. Fear took over as the doctors tried to discover the cause of the severe jaundice.

*The Miracle Baby* 3

Four days after Verlinda's birth, my blood was retested, and we learned that it was Rh-negative after all. Henry's and Verlinda's was positive. This meant that our baby's blood had become a battleground of harmful antibodies which had developed in my bloodstream and hers during the pregnancy.

The doctors were distressed. Had they known I was Rh-negative they would have prepared for a complete exchange transfusion had there been any sign of antibodies in her blood. To avoid damage, an exchange transfusion must be done within hours of birth. Now it was too late.

The agony continued as Verlinda struggled against a high fever, a bloodstream infection, and the severe jaundice. On December 22 the doctor reported that Verlinda was critically ill and suggested a blood transfusion. She was very listless by this time, and her hemoglobin had dropped to 30 percent.

During the administration of the blood transfusion, which was done by cutting into the vein in her ankle, Verlinda stopped breathing. She was resuscitated for about four minutes while bloody mucous was aspirated from her throat. The following day her breathing stopped again, and once more she was aspirated and resuscitated. Her chart reported her as an "acutely ill, deeply jaundiced newborn."

Christmas morning found me still in the hospital—another day of pain and anxiety as Verlinda continued to fight for life. I was awakened very early that morning by the sound of voices singing Christmas carols. I left my bed to open the door and saw the student nurses walking through the halls by candlelight. Hearing the familiar, much-loved songs lifted my spirits.

I can't remember now why I was not dismissed from the hospital to spend Christmas at home with my family. Perhaps I didn't want to go. Surely it would have been better to be sharing Christmas with Henry and the children, not only for my emotional needs but also for theirs.

Henry tried to make everything as normal and happy as possible for Anne and young Henry. Anne remembers that her father asked her at bedtime, "Well, Missy, how did I do today without Mummy here?"

She answered, "It was all right, but I didn't get my parrot." She told us that recently, and we laughed because we don't remember ever hearing about her wanting a parrot. Maybe it was because Henry, Jr., found a puppy under the tree for him.

On the day after Christmas, Verlinda's condition remained critical. The doctors were concerned that she might have a hepatitis-type infection, one which had shown up in another hospital causing the death of several babies. On January 4 a bone marrow test confirmed their fears.

The degree of jaundice continued to be very intense. The doctors were not able to say with certainty what was causing the severe jaundice. Was it erythroblastosis, the Rh factor incompatibility? Was it hepatitis, or was it some congenital deformity of the bile duct?

A surgeon was called in. His opinion was that there was not enough evidence of obstruction to warrant an operation. The doctors continued to give transfusions and decided that the jaundice was due primarily to liver damage.

Verlinda continued her fight to survive. On January, 9, 1947, she seemed to be momentarily improving. She took some fluids by mouth and appeared to be less jaundiced. However, she developed a rash on her thigh and leg from an infection surrounding the "cut-down."

On January 11 her temperature continued to be elevated, her color was poor, and her blood count dropped again. By the thirteenth she was much worse, and the rash spread to her scalp and chest. Another transfusion was given—the last one as it turned out.

January 15 brought the first positive statement on her chart: "There is improvement." The jaundice was lessening, and Verlinda was eating well. She was able to be out of the oxygen tent without becoming cyanotic (turning blue).

On January 30 the doctor finally stated that he could "see no reason why the infant could not go home."

We rejoiced in our "miracle baby" and at the prospect of having our family intact again.

# 2

# Descent into Darkness

*The land of gloom and chaos,
where light is as darkness.*
JOB 10:22

On a cold and snowy February 3, 1947 we brought Verlinda home. She weighed six pounds and ten ounces and had made medical history: nobody had expected her to live.

For awhile after we brought Verlinda home, we continued to treat her as a hospital patient, recording her temperature, her weight, the amount of formula and water she received, when she slept, how long it took her to eat, etc. The training and experience I had received as a Red Cross nurse's aide during the war was helpful. I felt efficient and capable and was thankful to be doing something for my baby.

One of the nurses who had been on night duty at the hospital came to our home to care for Verlinda at night. Verlinda was difficult to feed, and it sometimes took more than an hour to give her three ounces of liquid. Her temperature was erratic, and she was generally very fretful. We found it difficult to relax and treat her normally. Because she had difficulty sleeping and was restless, the doctor prescribed Phenobarbital. This helped her rest but made her very drowsy during her feeding. I wrote on the chart one day that she was "acting like a baby." It must have been the first time she seemed normal to me.

As the days and weeks went by, Verlinda made some physical progress, gaining weight, eating soft foods, and drinking larger amounts of formula and juice. However, there was no change in her response to us, no alertness, no lifting of her head when she lay on her stomach.

Her doctor, Bob Nix, was concerned, and so were we. He told us that the chances of her developing normally were very slim. He reviewed all her illnesses that could have caused brain damage—the jaundice and the anemia and the lack of oxygen to the brain during the time she had stopped breathing.

I couldn't imagine what it meant. I was still too caught up in Verlinda's recovery from what the doctors had considered a fatal illness. Perhaps he was wrong about this, and she would fool them again.

We decided to get another opinion, so Bob contacted the head pediatrician of Children's Hospital in Pittsburgh. We knew him and felt he would not mind coming to the house to see the baby. I was certain that he would come up with some ideas to help Verlinda develop.

He examined Verlinda, then told me, "I'm afraid the baby is never going to grow mentally. There's nothing we can do for her. I'm sorry."

I was crushed. "How far do you think she'll go?" I asked.

"She'll always be an infant."

"You mean just like she is now?"

"Oh, she might grow in some ways beyond where she is now, but it would be very slight."

I couldn't take it in. A grown-up infant was something I had never thought about, except for those people in huge state institutions. This was worse than anything Bob Nix had suggested to us. I hadn't suspected from what he had said that Verlinda would always be a baby. Slow maybe, but an infant forever?

And then the pediatrician made his most shattering statement. "We refer to this type of infant as one with a 'tower-shaped head,'" he said.

Visions of monsters filled my mind, and I fell apart inside. "Oh, God," I cried to myself, "what is he talking about? Is she going to look like some kind of freak when she gets bigger?" All I could see was a huge towering head—our baby, our miracle baby who had survived against such terrible odds.

It was obvious that the doctor was sorry to be the bearer and confirmer of such bad news. I was in a daze as I continued to do the things for Verlinda that needed to be done.

I went to the kitchen. The bottles and nipples had to be sterilized, so I put them on the stove to boil and went upstairs. Verlinda's room was directly above the kitchen, and it wasn't long before I smelled the odor of burning rubber. I raced downstairs and found the nipples a melted mass of rubber in the saucepan. I put more of them in another saucepan and went again to look at Verlinda. Maybe I could see something the doctor had missed, some spark that would prove him wrong.

Once again the house filled with the odor of burning rubber. "How am I going to stand this?" I thought. "What do you do when you are told, 'There is no hope'?" I felt as though I was in the middle of a nightmare with no way out.

I thought of the joy I had felt during my pregnancy—that won-

*Verlinda at two-three months*

derful time of creating. I lived those months with the anticipation of new life, the enlarging of our family, a future mystery waiting to be revealed. I had wondered what the baby would be like; would the child look like Anne or be more like Henry? I had looked forward to when the baby herself would be a creative being.

Now there was nothing. The family was enlarged, to be sure, but that baby lying on the bed would never create anything except heartache for us. I picked her up and sat in the rocker and rocked her back and forth. Her beautiful hands, her soft gray eyes, her wispy, blond baby hair and sweet face. In so many ways she seemed normal, like a living doll. As the years passed, we began to call her "Dolly." Ironically, she was never able to respond to us much more than a doll might.

I descended into fear. "What do we tell people?" I wondered. "What do we do?" It was too awful to think about. Maybe it would go away. Maybe there was some treatment the doctors hadn't heard about. "God, where are you! Why are you punishing me like this?" I raged at the unfairness, the waste, the loss.

It was "a time for weeping" and I wept.

# 3

# What Will People Think?

*But God chose what is foolish in the world
to shame the wise, God chose what is weak in the world
to shame the strong.*
1 CORINTHIANS 1:27

I have often thought of this verse in relation to Verlinda and other severely retarded people. He has chosen them and works through them to bring others to Jesus Christ. Doesn't that "confound the wise"? I have seen people who are gifted in many ways, considered to be leaders in the world, intellectually superior, who are puzzled by the mentally retarded, unable to see them as anything but tragic stumbling blocks. If they believe in God, they wonder why he would permit that kind of suffering.

The subject is deeper than I can understand myself, and I no longer try. But I know the truth of that verse from 1 Corinthians because I, too, am one of the weak and foolish things he has chosen.

I was born in Sewickley, a town in western Pennsylvania, two blocks from St. Stephen's Church, where I was baptized, married, and deeply involved later in my life. When I was two years old we moved to nearby Edgeworth. "Vineacre" was a large, red brick house on two acres of big trees, grass, and gardens—plenty of space for us to enjoy, and my two sisters and I made the most of it.

My childhood was fun in many ways, yet I also developed a number of attitudes about myself that took their toll on my confidence and self-esteem. I was the last of the three Doyle girls who were always dressed alike and known as a group, not as individuals. My only unique feature was being the brown-eyed blond of the family. I could never get away from the idea that I was no more than a tag-a-long.

I was actually fearful of being different, but I fancied myself the tomboy of the threesome. I even remember praying every night that I would wake to find myself a boy—unique in a family of girls.

Inside I was anything but tough, and I abdicated my identity to Virginia, my next older sister. As we grew, I withdrew more and more from the responsibility of being myself or taking initiative in developing relationships or even trying to remember people's names. It was easier to let Virginia make the friends than to take the risk myself.

I had a strong family bond with my cousins, encouraged by the whole clan's annual visit to our grandparents' summer home on Long Island. We shared many good times there, and I have since realized how important it was to grow up as part of an extended family where three generations lived as one household for a part of every year.

But it wasn't always easy. As one of the youngest cousins, I dreaded the teasing. I never knew when I was going to be ridiculed for a mispronunciation or some statement that exposed my ignorance. I often wished that the floor would open up and swallow me. In self-defense I tried to be funny and looked for others' mistakes to laugh at. Through the years the Lord has had to deal with me to discourage that quality in me. The positive side of all of that, though, was the development of a quick wit and the ability to see the funny side of life and of myself.

My father suffered from asthma. Because of his illness, he retired from business when I was nine, and we moved from one place to another, searching for a better climate than the smoggy Pittsburgh atmosphere.

Changing schools each year created a shaky foundation for my education. We often entered a school after it had been in session for several weeks or even months, and it was difficult to overcome the fear of being among strangers. We found that we repeated some courses and missed others completely.

The year we moved to California I kept a Bible beside my bed, hidden so that no one would see it and laugh at me. I was frightened of the new school and having to meet new children. Every morning or at bedtime I would read a passage. I don't remember what I read, but I must have been comforted or I would not have risked what others might think.

When I was twelve, my sister Rebecca went off to boarding school. The next year Virginia left, too. My mother felt sorry for me because I'd been left behind, and so she taught me to drive the car. I had just turned fourteen at the time, and my self-esteem took a giant step forward. My sisters had not yet learned to drive.

Then in late October my parents and I moved to a small town in the mountains of North Carolina. We lived in an inn, and I attended a school run by two elderly sisters which was somehow connected to the inn.

That year was an exciting one for me. For the first time I was on my own. The school was very small—only two other children in my class and probably no more than a dozen in the entire school. There were others in the community who went to the regular school, and it wasn't long before I met them. I made friends quickly and enjoyed the longed-for popularity of a northern teenager among a group of southern peers.

The next year I also went to Westover, the boarding school in New England. I loved my three years there. Coming in as one of the "new girls" gave me the chance to make friends separate from those of my sisters.

At one point I asked my parents if I could attend a Christian conference founded by Dwight L. Moody for high school students, but my parents said no. They feared I might become overly religious. After graduating, I wanted to go to college. They looked into the idea but decided against it for fear that girls were allowed too much freedom at college.

These were minor set-backs during the years when many people were experiencing major ones as the Great Depression descended upon society. But they were *my* disappointments, and they colored my life, increasing my difficulty in making choices and knowing who I was.

I spent the years between high school graduation and marriage in a useless round of parties, singing lessons, a chorale group, volunteer work in a hospital, bridge, and golf—acceptable activities of the day. I lived in a selfish world of my own, always wishing things were different but not daring to take the risks to make them so.

Henry and I met in the summer of 1933. After graduation from Harvard and a trip around the world for a year, he returned to Pittsburgh, his hometown, to work in the family steel mill. He joined our crowd of friends.

I was living with my parents in Florida the winter of 1934–1935 (still searching for the best climate for my father), when Henry came down to ask for my hand in marriage. It was an exciting time, and we were very happy. We believed our marriage would be perfect. We decided to be married on June 29.

When I met Henry's family I fell into a state of terror. I was overwhelmed by the large staff of servants, the sophisticated lifestyle, and people who were very stylish and articulate. I discovered that my nervous system was located in my stomach, and for an entire weekend I was unable to eat.

For me, there was a fairy tale quality to this part of my life—the handsome prince, a Phi Beta Kappa Harvard graduate, and the shy, insecure, immature Cinderella. Henry and I planned to build a house on Dundee Farm, a property he had inherited from his aunt. After the wedding we were to take a two month honeymoon to the Mediterranean and other exotic places. Was it too good to be true? I didn't think so. I was certain that life would be perfect from that time on. Marriage would change me, and I would be somebody.

I didn't know that marriage cannot change a person on the inside anymore than moving to a new town could. I carried with me all the baggage that had been there from the beginning.

After our sail in the Mediterranean, our honeymoon took us through Italy (where I learned I was pregnant), Austria, Hungary, a day's trip on the Danube, to Germany, where I was introduced to my first opera, then France and England, our final stop.

Finally Henry and I settled down in our new house on Dundee Farm. We called it the "House at Pooh Corner" (one of my nicknames was Pooh) and looked forward to our baby's arrival in the spring.

The reality and goodness of this time entwined with a stubborn thread of insecurity and anxiety. It colored my experiences and relationships, and I lived life in a mist, not fully alive or aware of who I was.

Something always terrified me about being different: What will people think? Did the social system assume that everyone would do the same thing, wear the same clothes? Or was it just in my mind?

This concern accounts for much of the fear I experienced when we learned that Verlinda was "different." Somehow a child as badly damaged as she was didn't fit into the categories that enabled me to blend in. Could we do things other families could do? Would people be uncomfortable around us? Would people point and whisper?

The old phrase, "What will people think?" was one of the first thoughts to race through my mind even then.

# 4
# Trapped

*Lord, all my longing is known to Thee,
my sighing is not hidden from Thee.*
PSALM 38:9

Our daughter Anne was born in April, 1936. We had gone to see Charlie Chaplin in *City Lights* and laughed hard enough to bring on a speedy delivery a few hours later. Anne was a lovely, healthy baby, and her father and I were proud and happy.

During my stay in the hospital, I developed a high fever. Because of a breast infection, I was no longer permitted to nurse the baby. My hospital stay lasted three weeks, and so my mothering got off to a bad start. Once at home, a nurse came to take care of the baby.

Soon I began to feel trapped by having two servants in the house and a nursemaid as well. Yet I did not have the courage to change the arrangement. I was afraid to go against the expectations of my mother if the baby was not "properly" cared for or to risk what the Chalfant family would think if our home was not run according to Chalfant standards and custom.

Henry, Jr. arrived in January of 1940, and I was thankful that we had a son and heir to carry on the Chalfant name. We took more pleasure in parenting, and Henry was a happy baby. My cup was full.

It wasn't until Verlinda came that my values began to change. Before her illness and retardation, I was living superficially in the role of society wife and mother. I served on a hospital board and the board of a home for children from broken homes. I worked in a hospital clinic as a volunteer, belonged to a garden club, was on the board of the private school which Anne and Henry attended, and played golf well enough to make the second-string club team. We entertained, travelled, and were active in the church.

Many of these activities I enjoyed tremendously, and there were opportunities for creativity, especially in the garden club making lovely flower arrangements or creating small gardens for the annual Garden Market exhibit. I lived a life of ease, breakfasting in bed and taking to my bed at the slightest hint of illness or fatigue. Margaret, our nursemaid for the children, absorbed most of the work in caring for them.

My life appeared to be full and satisfying, but there was something missing. I knew that deep inside I wasn't happy. I thought, "If Henry and I moved away from Mother's watchful eye, we could start over. We wouldn't have a nurse for the children; I could be more independent and learn how to do something creative." Or: "If only Henry would get another kind of job—teaching someplace maybe—instead of being in business doing what everyone else is doing, then we could meet people from other backgrounds."

I wanted others to change or to change my environment. I couldn't see that *I* needed to change. If the thought ever occurred to

*Trapped*

me, I certainly didn't have the courage to do anything about it.

So when World War II came along and Henry was accepted for officers' training in the Air Force, I was certain that everything would be better. I pictured us moving away to a place where we would really live, away from the boundaries—both emotional and physical—of Sewickley, Pennsylvania.

Henry and I, the children, Margaret, and my mother were spending a short holiday in South Carolina when orders came from the Air Force for Henry to report to Miami for officers' training for a period of six weeks. I joined him there and remained until he received his orders. Henry was directed to report to Savannah, Georgia. We were thrilled, and our friends among the group of officers and their wives were envious of us. I had loved the South after living for two winters in the Carolinas. I believed that Savannah would be the ideal place.

We arrived in Savannah, and planned to go "house hunting" that afternoon. But Henry reported for duty and returned to the hotel with crushing news. He was to go overseas immediately. We couldn't believe it. Henry had no desire to leave his family so soon and was barely adjusted to military life. As for me, all my hopes had been wrapped up in moving away from Sewickley, and now I would have to go right back there—alone.

I wept all through dinner in the hotel that evening. Poor Henry! His going overseas and endangering his life was less threatening to me at the time than my having to go back home to Sewickley for the duration. After a 48-hour leave spent at home with the children, Henry left Fort Dix on June 14, 1942.

My life during the three years that Henry was overseas settled into a routine, and for all my initial grief, it was an interesting and fulfilling life in many ways. Since Margaret helped with the children, I was free to spend many hours as a Red Cross Nurse's Aide at Sewickley Hospital. The nurses were extremely busy, and much of the floor care was turned over to us.

I worked many evenings in the nursery for newborn babies. The nurse and I shared many heartaches in the years that followed—her two children born after the war were *both* severely handicapped.

Henry's tour of duty came to an end in the summer of 1945. Finally we could pick up our lives and once again plan to enlarge our family. I thought things would be different for us, that we had been given a second chance. We were both more mature after the experiences of the past three years. I hoped that Henry would find work in another part of the world or that perhaps we could develop our farm, making it a paying operation. I wanted to share together in a different kind of lifestyle. I dreaded the thought of drifting back to where we had been before the war.

But the months went by with no sign of an approaching pregnancy, and I resumed the old patterns of longing for other people to change and circumstances to be different. Once again I felt trapped in my negative emotions.

Is it any wonder that Verlinda's condition struck me with such force? I was hopelessly self-centered and emotionally immature and didn't seem to know how to grow up. It took the life of someone else to wake me up and start me growing. In a sense Verlinda laid down her life for mine.

# 5

# Loneliness

*The sun and the moon are darkened,
and the stars withdraw their shining.*
JOEL 3:15

The time between that grievous day when we were told that Verlinda's condition was hopeless and that she would never grow mentally beyond infancy and the day I came to know Jesus Christ was less than two years, but the living of it seemed endless to me.

Each morning I awakened with deep heaviness and a fear of what the day would bring. Could I handle the people who asked how Verlinda was getting along?

When she first came home from the hospital it was easy and exciting to report on whether she had gained weight or on how she had been eating and sleeping. She was our miracle baby, who survived a near-fatal illness.

As the news of her retardation became known, there were fewer and fewer who asked about her, a logical and understandable response on the part of friends. They were fearful of saying the wrong thing and did not want to offend us or cause us pain. But it built a barrier and stifled communication because the thing that was all-consuming in my life became a subject to be avoided.

I was grieving as deeply as if my child had died, and yet I had to go about as though life were normal. My heart broke each time I saw a normal, healthy baby. I forgot at what an early age babies developed different skills, and I was shocked and pained to see other babies making eye contact and responding with smiles and even laughter, or to note how they held up their heads, reached out for toys, and crept on their hands and knees.

I was touched when my sister gave me a set of oil paints because I knew that she wanted to provide an outlet for me, something to fill the emptiness and lack of creativity in a seemingly dead-end experience, the experience of having a baby who would never be creative herself. It was a thoughtful and loving gift.

Barriers continued to grow, and communication with others became more and more difficult. Life took on a more superficial nature. It was easier to suppress the anger, resentment, and fear surging beneath the surface. Under a calm exterior, I was close to tears much of the time.

Margaret had left after the war when I finally acquired the courage to say we no longer needed a nursemaid for the children. But when Verlinda was six months old, we invited her back to help with Verlinda's care. Henry and I went off to Mexico for a three-week vacation with the idea of picking up our married life again in some normal pattern. But new sights and experiences could not take away the pain and fear of the future that lay deep inside me. I returned to Sewickley with the same despair and hurt, continuing to live in a superficial manner, trying to enjoy life, to entertain and become involved again in the activities of the community.

Henry's work took him quickly back to his own interests, but I had nothing I cared about enough to stir up a consuming interest in anything. I was immersed in feeling sorry for myself as well as for Verlinda. By the grace of God our marriage survived the introduction of the "not normal" child into our "normal" world. We were not prepared for the emotions that followed and our reactions to Verlinda. Henry was a rock, and I was in pieces. I couldn't understand why he didn't react as I did.

Henry had a solid faith, and it carried him through the sorrow he felt over Verlinda. He would have done anything or gone anywhere to find help for her, but once he knew that there was nothing that could be done other than caring for her as best we could at home, he accepted it.

But my life didn't continue as before. The radical change presented a threat to a marriage relationship that had been created in one kind of world but was catapulted into a very different one. I felt alone. It was hard on both Henry and me.

Years later when I worked at the St. Peter's Child Development Centers, I was shocked by the number of broken homes in families with severely handicapped children; nearly four out of five don't make it.

The Christmas of 1947 stands out in my mind as the most difficult one of my life. It was Verlinda's first Christmas at home. We tried to find gifts for her that would arouse some response, but there was no wind-up toy, music box, or squeaky animal that broke through to her. I thought the day would be unbearable and we would be going through empty motions.

"Maybe the lights on the tree will attract her," I said to Henry, "or the train running around the track. It makes a lot of noise. There must be something that will make her smile or react in some way."

Christmas morning came, and the other children were excited

*Anne, Henry, and Verlinda*

and happy with their gifts. They offered the teddy bear they had gotten for Verlinda to her as she sat in Margaret's lap. She was unaware of it just as she was unaware of the bells we jangled in her ears, first one and then the other. Her gray eyes never tracked the bright Christmas lights. There were no smiles, no expressions on her unresponsive face.

Anne and Henry, Jr., weren't looking for a response from her, so they were not upset and went about opening their own presents, enjoying everything to the full. But my heart grew heavier and heavier. I thought of future Christmases when we would go through the same thing. "What do you give someone who will always be a baby?" I thought to myself. "You give stuffed animals, wind-up toys and pretty clothes to wear." Could I handle that for the rest of Verlinda's life, or mine?

"Last Christmas was bad enough," I thought. I was still in the hospital and Verlinda was dying, but at least there was the slight hope that she would survive. This year there was no hope, only years stretching ahead interminably, unchanging for Verlinda.

The Christmas of 1947 found me engrossed in sorrow. There seemed to be no light to lighten my darkness. Later, when I came to know Jesus Christ and had made some progress in my spiritual growth, I could see that much of my grief over Verlinda was self-pity. Naturally I grieved that she was not going to develop at a normal rate of growth, that she was not going to lead a normal life, and that she would be denied the activities that the rest of the family took part in; I grieved also for the loss of hopes and joys of child-rearing. But a good part of my sorrow was caused by the hurt to myself. I was embarrassed, I feared the future, and I was wounded by other people's lack of understanding. I felt let down by the medical profession. I craved enormous amounts of sympathy and was hurt when I did not get it.

I was so immersed in my own grief that I was unaware of the needs of other people. Anne was only ten years old when Verlinda was born, and I have since learned that at the beginning she blamed herself for Verlinda's condition. She felt that she had upset me by being naughty the day before I went to the hospital. I don't remember the situation myself, but she recalls that I begged her to behave and she wouldn't. She carried a dreadful weight of guilt for a long time while I was too deeply into my own feelings to check on how she was taking it.

I remember being so full of self-pity on the day after that Christmas that I was physically sick and spent the day in bed.

In my grief it was hard for me to realize that other people were not able to relate to my grief in the way I expected them to. It was not *their* emotions that were involved; it was only *mine*. My expectations were inordinately unrealistic at the time. I had to learn that each person's experience of grief and suffering is unique and cannot be fully shared by another person, no matter how close that person might be. My grief and sorrow were unique to me.

# 6
# The Turning Point

*Weeping may tarry for the night,
but joy comes with the morning.*
PSALM 30:5

At nearly two years of age, Verlinda could still look fairly normal at first glance . . . if she was calm. Her hair was blond and curly, her eyes gray, and her facial features favored mine. We always kept her nicely dressed. But already, one only had to watch her a few moments to realize she wasn't normal. Her eyes did not track or focus on anything. She could not hold her head up or make any other purposeful move—no sitting, no crawling, no holding on to things. Often her body was spastic, jerky, and uncontrolled. Her tongue worked continually, often not in her mouth. As time went on, she did not gain much weight. What little growing she did left her body thin and unsupported. It was hard to hold or carry her as she jerked into positions that certainly looked painful.

The task of caring for a perpetual infant was immense, and the emotional prospect of an unchanging future was overwhelming. My church and family background had not prepared me for the trial I was going through. To describe myself objectively, however, I must look back through the eyes of faith given to me by God when my heart was broken and I was no longer able to function in a "normal" world.

Those eyes of faith came to me as a gift through reading *The Healing Light* by Agnes Sanford, a new book published in 1947. This book was the turning point, the watershed of my life in the summer of 1948.

That summer I had been talking to my hairdresser, a Christian Scientist. She inquired one day about my family, and I told her about our three children, Anne, Henry, and Verlinda. "Verlinda is very handicapped. She's a year old, but she can't do anything. She's just like a newborn baby. She can't even hold her head up. The doctors say she doesn't even see or hear."

"What church do you belong to?" she asked. I wondered what that had to do with Verlinda, but I answered, "St. Stephen's. It's an Episcopal church."

"What does that church teach about healing?" she wanted to know.

"I don't know," I said, "I don't think it teaches anything about it. What do you mean?"

She began to tell me what the Christian Science Church believes. I knew a little about their beliefs but thought they were strange. I couldn't imagine being sick and not calling a doctor or taking medicine. They even refused to have bones set or be treated by doctors for any illness no matter how serious! "That would never be an option for me and my family," I thought. And yet as I saw her week by week and she spoke each time of examples of healing in people

*The Turning Point*

she knew, I began to listen. She gave me articles and books to read, and I became more and more interested in the healing power of God.

"Why doesn't our church teach these things?" I wondered. "It's in the Bible. Jesus spent a lot of time healing people with impossible problems, the crippled (Verlinda), the blind (Verlinda), the deaf (Verlinda). Couldn't he heal Verlinda?"

I began to hope: "Maybe what she is saying is true. Maybe if we invited a Christian Science practitioner to visit Verlinda it would help her. Surely there is no harm in trying."

I spoke to one of our ministers about it. I told him about my interest in Christian Science and asked, "What do you think?"

I'll never forget his answer: "This just isn't for you. You need to keep yourself so busy you won't have time to think about the day when you will have to put Verlinda in an institution."

I felt as though the bottom had dropped out of life again. Looking back now, I can understand his response better. He knew aspects of Christian Science about which I was ignorant, and he saw it as a disruptive force for our family and our life in the church. But at the time I felt that the professionals had let me down once again.

Where else could I turn? I was back in the dark where there was no hope, no healing. Healings happened 2,000 years ago when Jesus was alive, not now. Whatever made me hope that Verlinda could be helped? He was right—an institution would be the only outcome, not a healthy, normal child healed by God.

But my spirits rose when I remembered that Bishop Pardue from Pittsburgh had expressed an interest in Verlinda and had prayed for her when she had been so ill in the hospital. "I'll go to see him," I thought.

I wish that I could remember the exact date of my appointment with him because it marks the date of my spiritual birth. We sat in his office in Trinity Cathedral, and I told him about my interest in Christian Science.

We discussed that religion for awhile. "I don't agree with all of it," he said, "and it's not true to Christian faith as the Bible teaches us. Furthermore, I believe that God works through doctors and medicine in both physical and mental problems. But I know there is value in their commitment to healing."

He picked up a book from his desk and said, "I'd like you to read this book by Agnes Sanford. Her husband is an Episcopal minister. I know her, and she is a remarkable person."

The title, *The Healing Light*, sounded hopeful. I thanked him, we had a prayer together, and I left his office with a feeling of excitement and hope. I couldn't wait to get into that book, and as soon as dinner was over that evening I began to read. I didn't put it down until it was finished. Sometime during the night I felt an incredible warmth and joy filling me. I knew it must be God's power, the power of the Holy Spirit, because that was what Mrs. Sanford was writing about.

Oh, what hope I was filled with then! God's power was real, and I was actually feeling it as it burned in my heart. I knew that he loved me and Verlinda and wanted her to be whole and well. I saw that I could be a channel through which that power could work, and I didn't have to sit by helplessly as Verlinda grew in years but not in mentality. Jesus became real to me, no longer a shadowy figure living 2,000 years ago but a person to love and be loved *now*, *today*, a person who loved Verlinda, too, and who hurt when we hurt.

I realized with joy that I did not have to become a Christian Scientist to believe in God's healing power. There was no argument against the medical profession or the use of medicines or other treatments. God's healing power worked through them as well as through his direct healing. In her chapter on "Doctors, Ministers, and God," Mrs. Sanford said:

> In ninety-nine times out of a hundred the wise care of the doctor and our own perseverance in faith will raise us to life

again. There is, however, the hundredth time—the sudden and deadly infection that is beyond the doctor's power of healing or the slow and hidden deterioration that has exhausted the recreating power of the body. Is there anything more we can do? There is. The most powerful healing method of all, we have not yet tried: The method of dealing by the faith of someone else who acts as a receiving and transmuting center for the life of God . . . Jesus interposed His whole being between God and the patient, so that He might be used as a channel for the life of the Father, who alone, He said, accomplished the works. (Agnes Sanford, *The Healing Light*, St. Paul, MN: Macalester Park Publishing Company, p. 86.)

The book was filled with hope, and I, who had been living for more than a year without hope, felt such a weight taken from me that I went to bed that night with the love of God coursing through me. I awoke in the morning filled with unbelievable joy. It was the joy the psalmist wrote about. I wanted to shout from the housetops what had happened to me.

I was amazed to find that as I read the Bible, it took on new meaning and a reality I had never found before. It was filled with promises, positive promises, some that I had recently experienced such as: "Blessed are those who mourn, for they shall be comforted" (Matthew 5:4). I certainly knew the meaning of that; I was living it.

I began to memorize all the positive statements I could find: "Thou dost keep him in perfect peace, whose mind is stayed on thee" (Isaiah 26:3); "Come to me, all who labor and are heavy laden, and I will give you rest" (Matthew 11:28); "I can do all things in him who strengthens me" (Philippians 4:13); and my favorite—Psalm 91: "He that dwelleth in the secret place of the most High shall abide under the shadow of the Almighty . . ." (KJV). I knew the meaning of the secret place now because I was "dwelling" in it myself.

My depression and the feeling of living in limbo vanished. I had been turned around and was facing in a new direction. I had turned my eyes upon Jesus—as the song goes—and looked "full in his wonderful face; where the things of earth grow strangely dim, in the light of his glory and grace." I was living with hope where before there had been none. Finally there was something we could do—pray, believing in the power of God, knowing that there was meaning to prayer, that God was real, and he was willing to hear and answer, to guide and direct us.

My heart sang, and I praised and thanked him for making himself known to me! I was totally and radiantly in love, and every waking thought was centered on Jesus Christ. I was filled with a new joy, the fruit of the Spirit that only God can give, and I had lost all fear of what the future held. I knew in my mind, heart, and spirit that there was nothing to fear, that Jesus was all I would ever need.

I had had my "night of weeping"—the deepest kind of grief a person can know. But now I knew without any doubt what being "born again" meant. I was a new creation in Christ. "The old has passed away, behold, the new has come" (2 Corinthians 5:17).

# 7

# The Power of Prayer

*Come to me, all who labor and are heavy laden,
and I will give you rest.*
MATTHEW 11:28

*Shortly after reading* The Healing Light, *the book which opened my spiritual eyes to God's Word,* Bishop Pardue encouraged me to pray regularly with others, not just during Sunday worship but during the week as well.

I called a friend who had recently learned that her daughter, then about five years old, would be slow in her mental development. She expressed an interest in the bishop's suggestion that we meet for prayer and thought of another friend who had belonged to a prayer group before moving to Sewickley.

Our bishop met with us once or twice to get us started. He warned us of the dangers of becoming too involved in discussing the problems of the people we primarily should be praying for. "Keep your eyes and minds on Jesus Christ and not on the illness or whatever the problem might be," he cautioned. "And be careful that you don't get into an attitude of 'you scratch my back, and I'll scratch yours'! Keep looking out and up so that you don't become ingrown or exclusive."

Gradually our group increased in number. We began to meet weekly at St. Stephen's Church in the chapel there. Eventually our numbers increased enough to move us from the chapel to the church, where we continued to meet for many years.

We prayed always for our own retarded children and for others we came to know, and we prayed for many other concerns. We read and discussed books on prayer and healing as well as the Bible, and completed our time together with Communion.

It was the high point of my week. We were all experiencing the newness of life that Paul wrote about in Romans. We were hungry for spiritual food and were being fed. We wanted to share this blessing with others, and it wasn't long before we were asked to go to other churches in the Pittsburgh area to tell about our prayer group and how God had worked through the need of one handicapped child to show us how to put our trust in him. We spoke of the importance of two or three gathering together in Christ's name to pray, of the power of prayer, and of how we were growing in our relationships to Jesus Christ and to one another. We were able to give examples of answered prayer and to tell about changed lives and solved problems.

The most dramatic answer to prayer we experienced concerned the husband of one of our members. He was a professed atheist, but his wife came faithfully to our Thursday morning group. We received word one day that her husband had had a stroke and was in Sewickley Hospital seriously ill. Two of us met her at the hospital and prayed with her, trusting in God to heal her husband. All the members of the group were alerted to his condition, and we organized a prayer vigil so that throughout the next twenty-four hours one of us was always praying for him.

He recovered and during the time of his recuperation at home he made a cross of cherry wood for each of the members of the prayer group, about forty people. He became a believer, and the cherry wood cross was his way of thanking us. A card from his wife accompanied each cross:

> This cross of cherry wood was made by Hugh Replogle during his recent long convalescence. He has made a similar cross for each of us in the prayer group. His purpose in making these crosses is two-fold: first as a small thank-offering for complete recovery from a serious illness; and secondly, the cross is intended as a personal reminder for each of us of our self-dedication as a group to a program of daily intercessory prayer.

Hugh thanked God with his life. He resigned from his job at one of the Pittsburgh steel companies to study for the ministry. He was forty years old at the time of his stroke.

The Bible commands us to come to God with our needs. Jesus Christ came to tell us that God would hear and answer our prayers. He taught us how to pray. I had prayed perfunctory prayers as long as I could remember, from the time I was a small child. I had no concept of what praying really meant or of the God to whom I was praying.

Verlinda changed all that, or rather the Holy Spirit changed it through my despair over her and in answer to the prayers of others who knew the meaning of prayer. Once my eyes were opened by the Spirit and I saw who Jesus was, my prayers became real. I looked forward eagerly each morning to be up and in communication with my Father in heaven. I prayed without ceasing, without any effort.

I don't remember how long that time lasted. I wonder sometimes as I look back on it. "Why didn't it go on for the rest of my life—that kind of effortless prayer?" But now I recognize that those experiences are the milk Paul speaks of that we are fed on as baby Christians. Just as a baby has no responsibility for providing his own nourishment but just lies in his mother's arms and receives it, I rested in God's arms and received his gift of love. That love made desiring to be in communication with him completely effortless.

But the time came when I had to assume greater responsibility for my spiritual growth, in the same way children must assume responsibility for their actions. I began to have setbacks as I experienced antagonism and lack of understanding in others. Satan began to work on me, and I let myself be distracted by the duties that pressed in on me. It was no longer easy to get up early in the morning or to dash to my bedroom when I returned home in the afternoon for a time of prayer before dinner. I no longer prayed without ceasing without hard work and conscious effort.

Walking by faith is an ongoing discipline, and we are called to be obedient. The Israelites rejoiced at being freed from the power of Egypt and eagerly left behind the country where they had lived in bondage. They thanked God as they watched the waters of the Red Sea close over the pursuing Egyptians. Like the Israelites, I had been filled with joy and thanks when I was freed from the bondage of the world and my sins. But just as they found it difficult in the wilderness and longed for the comforts and riches of Egypt, there were also times when I found it hard to walk in faith with the freedom and joy I had known in the beginning.

Now, many years later, I see more clearly God's hand in all parts of my life. He has never forsaken me, and I know from experience that he never will. He was always ready to receive me when I was ready to return to him in prayer.

As we continued with our prayer ministry, Bishop Pardue continued to support us. He was interested in the ministry of healing and invited Agnes Sanford and Dr. Glenn Clark to speak at Trinity Cathedral in Pittsburgh. Dr. Clark was a professor of English at Macalester College in Minnesota. I had read his books on healing and prayer: *How to Find Health Through Prayer, The Soul's Sincere Desire,* and others, so I was delighted when he came to our home to pray for Verlinda. Through him I heard about the Camps Farthest Out, the spiritual retreats he conducted throughout the country.

In October of 1948 I learned that one of these retreats was being held nearby. I packed up Margaret and Verlinda for a week of concentrated prayer and teaching given by several leaders in the healing movement. Among them was Dr. John Gayner Banks, founder of the Order of St. Luke (the healing branch of the Anglican and Episcopal Church). He became interested in Verlinda and was very helpful to me. Father John (I thought of him as my spiritual father) became a dear friend and often came to visit us after that conference.

Verlinda didn't receive a healing at the retreat, but it was a great blessing to me—a time for growing spiritually, committing myself more deeply to follow the Lord, and feeling less strange in my newfound faith. I saw others there being healed of various illnesses and received a physical healing myself. My faith took a giant leap forward as I listened and watched others who had committed their lives to Christ and were full of the abundant joy he promised us.

# 8
# All Things Are Possible

*For he will give his angels charge of you
to guard you in all your ways.*
PSALM 91:11

Living by faith was a new experience for me. I rejoiced that I was a child of God, that I was part of a divine plan. I met other people of faith, and we strengthened one another as we prayed together.

Where I had been without hope and walking in the dark, I was now walking in the light. It had seemed that a door was slammed in my face as a result of Verlinda's handicap, shutting out everything that I had known before, but another door had opened, and I had walked through it. Hope was restored, and hopelessness and fear were gone.

Hope is a God-given quality, and trying to live without it is a denial of him. Was it any wonder, then, that I had rebelled when we were first told there was no hope for growth in Verlinda's mental development? The gift of hope within us will not surrender so quickly. Henry and I felt compelled to take Verlinda to other doctors, seeking someone with an answer to keep our hope alive. But over and over again we heard, "There's nothing we can do. Verlinda will remain an infant all her life." Hope was submerged.

Mrs. Sanford's book told me I could begin to hope again because God had given me this quality, and it was my responsibility to cultivate it. Through prayer it began to grow and develop into faith. As I prayed for greater faith, I began to see that "with God all things are possible" (Matthew 19:26).

God wants us to hope and to grow in faith. Doctors who believe in the power of God, who are continually on the alert for medical discoveries, and who are willing to try new methods of therapy are the ones through whom God can work. Let them pray for guidance, and let them help parents keep the gift of hope alive.

Any situation surrounded by prayer, faith, hope, and love becomes creative. It was not long before my gift of faith was tested.

Much to our amazement, when Verlinda was a little more than three years old, I became pregnant. Ever since Anne's birth I had had difficulty conceiving a child. Before Henry's birth I had gone through the usual procedures of taking shots, etc. and had even resorted to major surgery.

This time there was no thought of taking to my bed as I had during my pregnancy with Verlinda. I believed that with the healing power of God I was experiencing there would be no danger of losing the baby. I was completely free of fear. I believed that if God wanted me to have a physically and mentally healthy baby, I would have one.

I decided not to see a doctor until after a visit from Father John Banks. I wanted him to bless the baby I was carrying before any doctor told us about the risks that were involved.

Father John lived in California, but he traveled a great deal conducting healing missions throughout the country. He was free during that week in April and had expressed a longing to relax with our family and have some quiet time.

Father John didn't expect to be entertained, although we did have some friends in for tea one afternoon. We learned something of his disciplines. He awakened at four o'clock in the morning to spend an hour or two in prayer. In the afternoon he rested. He enjoyed walking around the farm, and we had many opportunities to talk. I soaked up his counsel and advice.

I can best describe Father John as a person "in whom there is no guile," and we all enjoyed his delightful sense of humor. Only Anne resisted the friendship. He represented a threat to her—a threat to the way of life she understood. "I hated him," she told me years later. "I hated everything that had happened to make you different, and he was part of that. And I thought his jokes were awful," she added. It was a natural reaction for a teenager wanting to be sophisticated. I suspect that if he had not died a few years later, she would have learned to see him differently.

During that visit Father John blessed my unborn child, and, on Easter Sunday before his visit ended, he received me into the Order of St. Luke in a brief induction service in our living room. Father John had dedicated himself to bring back the teaching and practice of Jesus and his power to heal to the church. The Order of St. Luke the Physician was an outgrowth of his commitment.

I made the resolutions required of members—to pray daily for the work of the Order, to read from the Gospels daily, and to share the Healing Gospel with others by personal witness. As I made these commitments, I felt the assurance of God's love for me and the promise of a healthy baby.

Immediately after Father John's visit, I resolved to see the doctor about my pregnancy. But the morning after he left I woke up feeling miserable—with fever and swollen glands. Anne and Henry, Jr., had both recently recovered from mumps. I thought I'd had mumps as a child, so I had assumed I was immune. I was wrong! The doctor confirmed that I had the mumps, and I was ordered to bed. What a way to begin my membership in the Order of St. Luke!

The illness did give me a lot of time to read and pray, and, perhaps it was God's way of keeping me quiet during that crucial time.

On the seventeenth of April I wrapped a scarf around my swollen neck and came downstairs to celebrate Anne's fourteenth birthday. During dinner Margaret called down that Verlinda was having a severe convulsion. She had just started having these. Her eyes blinked rapidly, and her whole body twitched and jerked. Usually the convulsions lasted for less than fifteen minutes, and if she were in her braces and on her bed, she did no harm to herself. I ran upstairs to give her the prescribed injection of sodium luminol, but she didn't respond to it, and the seizure continued for more than an hour.

The doctor came, examined her, and suggested that she had pneumonia and would be better off in the hospital. Henry and Margaret took her, while Anne, her brother, and I finished the birthday celebration alone. Though in many ways Henry did not engage himself in the day-to-day care of Dolly, he was nonetheless supportive and always there in an emergency or when important decisions needed to be made. He went off to spend the first of many nights at the hospital with Verlinda as she once again fought to live. Her temperature rose to 107 degrees, and she was not expected to pull through.

When she did come home more than three weeks later, we established a hospital routine again, working in three shifts. The nurse that had cared for her at the hospital continued at home with her at night. Margaret went on duty for the morning shift, and I took over the afternoon and evening. I am amazed at the records we kept. I forget now how very sick she was and for how long a time she was restless and unaware, sleeping very little and crying constantly. She received phenobarbital three times a day and other medication to keep the seizures under control. By the middle of July we saw improvement, and she began to gain a little weight and respond with occasional smiles. It had been a difficult time.

Through all this I seemed to be doing very well physically. I had been assured by the doctor that lifting Verlinda in her braces would not be harmful as long as I had been accustomed to doing it. I was taking weekly injections of a serum that was supposed to prevent the build-up of antibodies in my blood, the effects of Rh-positive blood entering my Rh-negative bloodstream. The doctor promised that the baby would receive a complete transfusion if there were any signs of erithroblastosis. I was not afraid. Faith and fear cannot live in the same place, and God's promises continued to be very real to me.

The baby was due in mid-November, and I looked forward to a natural delivery. But on the morning of October 14 the unexpected happened. I was getting ready to take Anne and her dog to the annual dog show when I began to bleed profusely. I called the doctor, and he said to get to the hospital as quickly as possible and he would be there to meet me. He sounded concerned. I didn't know that my problem was a placenta previa, a condition that in itself could cause either death or brain damage to the baby because it cuts off oxygen to the brain.

Henry was in Canada for some grouse shooting with a friend. I caught my sister and her husband on their way to a football game, and they promised to get me to the hospital.

While I waited I explained to Anne that we couldn't go to her dog show. She said excitedly, "I'll pack your suitcase for the hospital, Mum. Oh, how exciting! I wonder if it's going to be a boy or a girl." I was touched by her enthusiasm. She gathered my things together, and I was ready to go.

My sister and brother-in-law drove me to the hospital in record time. As we pulled up to the door, I remembered all that had happened at the hospital the last time I was there as a patient. "This time will be different," I said to myself. "That was before I knew the Lord, and now I know that the baby and I are in his hands, and he wants the best for us."

The doctor was waiting for me when they took me up to my room. "I'll have to do a Caesarean section right away," he said. "So much for the natural childbirth exercises," I thought. I was disappointed but not frightened at the urgency of the operation.

The spinal anesthetic made me a bit groggy, but I saw the doctor lift the baby out and heard him say, "It's a girl." She looked a little blue, but the doctor assured me she was fine. I wasn't surprised. That gift of faith was working overtime!

Back in my room I lay thinking how wonderful it was to have another little girl. I thanked and praised God for the blessing she would be to all of us. The contentment I had felt when Verlinda was born was all there but was enhanced by the dimension of faith and love for Jesus Christ that had given me a new heart and mind.

The baby was three hours old when the doctor told me that she needed the complete exchange transfusion. "She'll have to have it done at Children's Hospital because we're not equipped to do it here. Your brother-in-law said he would drive the baby there—with a nurse, of course."

"Oh, I wish she didn't have to go to another hospital," I said. "I won't be able to nurse her." I experienced disappointment but again remembered God's faithfulness and was thankful that the doctors at the other hospital had the special skills needed to protect our baby.

Soon after Charles got to Children's Hospital with the baby, he called. "What's the baby's name?"

"I don't know," I said. "We hadn't decided on a girl's name. Let's see, Henry and I talked about Isabella, for Henry's aunt, or maybe Nancy, but we hadn't decided definitely."

"Well," he said, "they seem to have to know right away, so I'll tell them her name is Nancy."

I was pleased. I had a namesake.

*All Things Are Possible*

The transfusion was successful. There were no complications. Nancy weighed six and a half pounds at birth, so, even though she arrived four weeks ahead of schedule, she was off to a good start. They kept her in an incubator at Children's Hospital for two weeks. She faced another setback when a hot water bottle filled with overly hot water was placed in her bed, and she received a second degree burn. She had to have intravenous medication of sulphanilamide to prevent infection, a drug that can sometimes cause deafness.

But God's love didn't fail us. Nancy grew and developed in every way as a healthy child. She was a joy to the family, and I felt I had been given a chance to raise a child from the beginning to know and love the Lord.

I still praise and thank God for the gift of faith he gave me during that particular time in my life. Without it I doubt if I could have withstood the negative events of my pregnancy, Nancy's birth, and the early days of her life. Instead of becoming alarmed, agitated, or terrified that she might be handicapped like her sister, I trusted in God's will for her wholeness. It was more than "positive thinking"; it was a deep trust in God.

The Bible is full of comforting words about trust. The one that meant the most to me at that time was Psalm 91. I allowed its healing words to live in me and rested in them. The flow of this psalm in the King James Version brings peace and comfort each time I recall it.

> He that dwelleth in the secret place of the most High shall abide under the shadow of the Almighty.
> I will say of the Lord, He is my refuge and my fortress: my God; in him will I trust.
> There shall no evil befall thee, neither shall any plague come nigh thy dwelling.
> For he shall give his angels charge over thee, to keep thee in all thy ways. (Psalm 91:1-2, 10-11, KJV)

# 9
# Light in the Darkness

*The light shines in the darkness,
and the darkness has not overcome it.*
JOHN 1:5

A mother never quite forgets that once she carried her child within her. During the pregnancy her physical body was busy creating the physical body of her baby, while her mind and heart were creating plans and dreams about what the baby would be like, what he would do, and what a joy he would be to the rest of the family. A mother is full of hopes for the baby's physical health and wholeness, and she eagerly anticipates the addition of a new personality to the family circle. Although the thought of physical or mental disability might enter her mind during that time, she would most likely put it out of her thoughts before it had any reality to her.

But when those dreams and hopes are torn away, a mother faces despair; they were too much a part of her to dismiss easily. Many parents of handicapped children have gone through the experience of being reminded of smashed hopes. It often happens when we see a child who is the same age as ours. We look at the child and can hardly believe that he has made so much progress. We have begun to adjust to and accept our own child, then it hits us again with a force that is overwhelming. It can send us back to the beginning, to face the same emotions and fears again.

These instances became more and more fleeting as time passed, and the impact on my emotions became less powerful as my faith in God increased. Certainly I did not feel the same sadness when I saw a group of sixth-grade children with whom Verlinda would have been associated had she progressed normally, as I felt when I had seen those same children in Kindergarten or the first grade. I no longer compared Verlinda to these other children as I had when she was two or three years old. I still thought, "These are the children who would have been Dolly's friends," but I didn't experience the same deep level of pain.

Now I see these young men and women in their thirties, and I think back to the pain and fear I knew when they were babies. Some have brought joy to their parents and lead productive lives, but others have brought only heartache. Had we all been able to see into the future, Verlinda's life could have been seen as less of a heartbreak than that of the young man who became addicted to alcohol and drugs and almost threw his life away.

As the years went by those things I had feared would be intolerable to go through year after year—the milestones of birthdays and succeeding Christmases—became opportunities to reach out to others.

For Verlinda's second birthday I baked a cake for another two-year-old who was born the day before Verlinda. God was beginning to use us both. By that birthday and Christmas I had come to know the Lord, and thus I responded differently to Verlinda's inability to notice the gifts and bright wrappings. I recognized the change in me. I was beginning to accept her as she was and was to enjoy the little indications of pleasure she was expressing. Sometimes she smiled when she saw lighted candles.

We celebrated some of her birthdays at the Watson Home for Crippled Children, where Verlinda went for therapy. These occasions were special because I knew that everyone accepted her and her limitations and loved her as she was. In their speech therapy program, some of the children were learning to blow, so there was a great deal of huffing and puffing as they tried to blow out the candles. What fun we had together! There is no group of people more full of fun than those with severe handicaps who have accepted themselves and others just as they are.

Nancy, our youngest, shared in some of these experiences. Anne and Henry, Jr., were away at school by that time, but Nancy was still at home. Verlinda was always part of her life. She used to spend a lot of time in Verlinda's room listening to records and playing quietly. "I always had a sense of peace when I was in Dolly's room," she remembers, "and I loved being in there with her and with you or Margaret when she was being fed. It was a peaceful and secure feeling. I don't ever remember being frightened of or embarrassed about her."

I recall a time when Margaret received a difficult phone call. One of Nancy's friends had spent the afternoon with her, and Margaret had taken them along when she and Verlinda went for their walk. That evening the mother of the little girl telephoned and said, "Please don't ever take my daughter out walking with Verlinda again." I was stunned. At the time I thought it was the reaction of a narrow-minded mother, but now I realize that it could have been the request of a little girl who felt uncomfortable being seen with someone who was so different.

In either case it could have been an opportunity for the mother to educate the child, to point out that children like Verlinda are

50                                                    *Child of Grace*

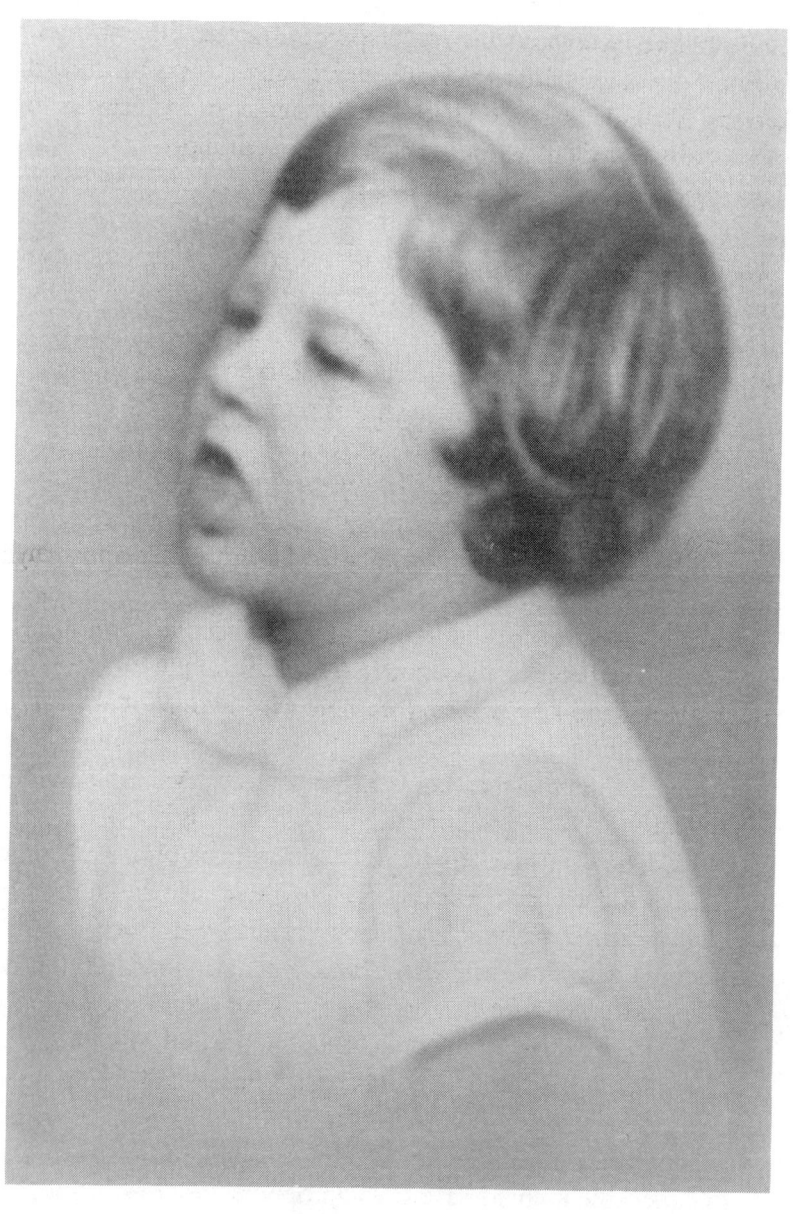

*Verlinda, five years old*

God's children who need love and respect as much as the rest of us.

Some of our friends had difficulty seeing anything positive in our keeping Verlinda at home. They felt the family would have been better off had we kept her out of sight in an institution somewhere. They viewed her only as a cloud over the lives of the rest of the family.

I am thankful that Nancy didn't see it that way. One day when she was quite young, she was considering Verlinda's illness and the miracle of her recovery when Verlinda had been so sick as a baby. When I remarked that Verlinda's life was a blessing and had a purpose, Nancy was already aware of this and listed several blessings—the blessing of people in our lives whom we would never have known if it hadn't been for Dolly, the blessing of knowing other children with handicaps. "And just think, if it hadn't been for Dolly we would never have known how they *feel*." My daughter spoke my heart as well.

Nancy is married now with three children of her own. I marvel at her patience and energy and wonder, for all my longing to care for my children without help when they were small, would I have managed?

Henry, Jr. was nearly six years old at the time of Verlinda's birth and was not very aware of our grief. That first Christmas after Verlinda's birth he received a puppy and was busy loving Wags.

He accepted Dolly from the beginning and never experienced any notable conflicts about her. He and his friends seemed unconcerned that Verlinda was different. They'd ask questions about her and were satisfied with the answers he gave them. "I was proud that our family was different," he once said. He was always loving toward Verlinda and ready to help Margaret and me with lifting and carrying her.

Henry feels that Verlinda's life broke into our constraining world of a society where both branches of his family had lived for three generations. Through the years, his freedom from that constraint has brought him many friendships with people from other countries and cultures.

Verlinda's condition was hardest on Anne. She was ten years old when Verlinda was born. I mentioned before that, for some time, she thought Verlinda's condition was her fault because she'd been naughty the day before I went into the hospital.

Anne, who has made her career in counseling, told me recently that, as the oldest child, she considered herself responsible for Verlinda's care if anything had happened to Henry and me. I was quite surprised. Henry and I had made provision for Dolly to be taken care of for the rest of her life. What a burden Anne carried all those years, and I hadn't realized it.

As a teen, Anne struggled with feelings of embarrassment about Verlinda. "She looked so different," Anne recalls. "Margie would be walking her along the road, and Verlinda would be sitting with her tongue lolling out. My friends would ask, 'What's wrong with her?'"

Henry and I just didn't discuss these things with the children very often.

I mentioned before that a psychologist had advised us to keep Verlinda at home lest Anne and Henry, Jr. feel insecure or fear that we might do the same to them. When Anne was about twelve, I tested the idea by asking how she would feel if we put Verlinda in a home somewhere. Anne burst into tears and said, "But Dolly is used to us. We love her, and she wouldn't be happy away from home!"

I'm afraid I assumed her response expressed the whole range of her feelings about Verlinda. I rejoice that Anne and I have a loving and understanding relationship. I wish I could have helped her adjust to our family situation when she was younger.

No doubt Verlinda's life *was* a cloud over each of us at times and in different ways, but I think the blessings outweighed the cloud and were opportunities for us to grow and expand our horizons. I prefer to see it from the same perspective as Pearl Buck, the 1938 Nobel prize-winning author and daughter of missionary parents in China, who was also the mother of a retarded child.

In 1959 I heard her speak to the Parents and Friends of the Mentally Retarded in Pittsburgh. Mrs. Buck emphasized the growth of a parent. She stressed again and again the importance of keeping our children at home as long as possible. To put them in an institution right away, as we are so often advised to do by the medical profession or well-meaning friends and relatives, deprives us of learning to love these children, of accepting them as they are, and of giving them the opportunity to be loved and surrounded by their families.

She pointed out that it is a blessing to the other children in the family, as well as their friends, to keep the retarded or handicapped child in the family circle. "Our American children," she said, "are too sheltered, and we deprive them of the opportunity of growing and becoming mature people when we try to shut life away from them."

There are many instances when it is impossible for a family to keep a handicapped child at home, but when it can be done, the process of growth begins.

While Mrs. Buck was speaking to us, I kept thinking, "Yes, that's exactly the way it was." Step by step Mrs. Buck brought us past the milestones of growth and acceptance as parents: the first terrible grief, the refusal to believe it, the refusal to lose hope, the searching from one doctor to another, the concern about what is right for the other children, and finally the acceptance of the handicapped child as she is, finding joy in the few signs of progress.

Mrs. Buck confirmed that with acceptance our hearts could reach out to do something for other handicapped children. "Then," she said, "we have turned away from the sadness of our own problem and can work toward a program of education, understanding, and help for all children with similar problems."

Pearl Buck spent much of her life as an advocate for the retarded. It was a privilege to hear her speak and to share the deep feelings that she expressed in her talk. I came away knowing that it is better to suffer and grow as a person than to avoid pain when it comes.

I had learned to take my sorrow and self-pity to God and in so doing learned the truth of the beatitude, "Blessed are those who mourn, for they shall be comforted" (Matthew 5:4). That verse had become a very real promise to me. I realized that God in his great mercy had taken my mourning and comforted me through knowing him and by giving me friends who, by their own experience of suffering, knew what I was feeling. I was also learning that all who suffer deeply can become "wounded healers" and bring comfort and understanding to others who are in the midst of sorrow or loss.

Paul writes:

> Praise be to the God and Father of our Lord Jesus Christ, the Father of mercies and God of all comfort, who comforts us in all our affliction, so that we may be able to comfort those who are in any affliction with the comfort with which we ourselves are comforted by God. For as we share abundantly in Christ's sufferings, so through Christ we share abundantly in comfort too (2 Corinthians 1:3-5).

Although I had reached a place of acceptance, there were times when my frustration level was very low, and I would be angry at God. I remember one night in particular. Margaret was on vacation and I had been sleeping in her room, adjacent to Verlinda's, for several nights. Most of those nights Verlinda had been very restless, and I had been up and down trying to quiet her.

On this particular night she was like a steel spring, all motion and very rigid. She writhed and jerked, stiffening and crying. Nothing I did quieted her. I put her in a warm bath and then wrapped her in a big towel and rocked her back and forth in the rocking chair as I sang hymns. I repeated the twenty-third Psalm again and again.

Nothing had any effect. I came close to snapping and pictured myself doing some harm to her. I put her back into her bed and got down on my knees, sobbing in anger at God.

"You promised," I cried. "You promised that if we had faith we could move mountains. You said when two or three were gathered together our prayers would be answered. Where are you? Why don't you even answer my prayer for Dolly to be quiet tonight? Why haven't you healed her? You promised! I don't believe you anymore. I hate you!"

Gradually I became still and cried quietly. I began to thank him for keeping me from harming Dolly.

It was a desperate time. I believe many parents of severely handicapped children go through something like that, but I know I couldn't have lived with myself afterward if I hadn't known God's forgiveness. I am thankful that I believed in a merciful and loving God, a God who promises that he will be with us, even though we "walk through the valley of the shadow of death" (Psalm 23). I know that he was with me that night, loving me in spite of my anger at him and at Verlinda, that in his mercy he forgave me and gave me the strength and compassion to go on.

A life lived in Jesus Christ is a life of continuing growth. Of course the goal of all Christians is perfection. Jesus said, "You, therefore, must be perfect, as your heavenly Father is perfect" (Matthew 5:48), and Paul echoed the same: "Be perfect" (2 Corinthians 13:11, KJV).

However, only Jesus is perfect, and although through the power of God's spirit we mature in Christ, it is not an instant maturity. We carry the baggage of spiritual and emotional sin and ignorance of God's laws. We shed pieces of our past one by one as the truth about ourselves is revealed to us.

By God's mercy we do not receive it all at once. We discover that our Christian walk is acknowledging the presence of the Lord with us moment by moment, and making those choices and decisions that please him.

With Paul we can say, "Not that I have already obtained this [becoming like Jesus] or am already perfect; but I press on to make it my own, because Christ Jesus has made me his own" (Philippians 3:12).

# 10
# The Door

*I am the door; if any one enters by me,
he will be saved, and will go in and out
and find pasture.*
JOHN 10:9

When the realization that Verlinda's condition was hopeless hit me fully, I walked through a door marked, "Retardation: Enter at Your Own Risk." I could have chosen to remain outside. We could have put Verlinda in an institution and, as some doctors advised, forgotten that we had had her. We could have gone on living as before, denying the existence of "The Door" and all that was on the other side.

But thank God, we chose to open it, and there on the other side was the new life which had been calling to me for so many years. I could never be the same again, and even though there were times when I longed to go back through the Door, I knew there was no going back.

On the other side of the Door I saw that many people were suffering as I was—mothers experiencing the same kind of sorrow, some handling it much better than I was.

These people were so real. For the first time in my life I found I could be real, too. There were no social barriers; we were all concerned about one thing: our retarded children. We laughed over them and cried over them. We didn't have to pretend. We shared the deep places of sorrow, and we shared, too, the brightest kind of joy.

God was there in our midst just as he promised he would be. Where all hope had been crushed at the first opening of the Door marked "Retardation," now there was hope and love. We loved one another's children as God loves them and we thought of ways to help them and each other. We were no longer part of the normal world—that was back on the other side of the Door.

You leave the normal world behind you when you live in a family which includes a severely handicapped child. You may try hard to hold on to the old patterns and to keep things the way they were for the sake of the family, but the reality is that you no longer *are* a normal family. At first it seems so frightening—we aren't prepared in any way for the abnormal.

Since shortly after our marriage, Henry and I had been living in the "House at Pooh Corner," the dream house we had planned and built on the corner of Dundee Farm. But as time went on, it was apparent that Verlinda would need special space and equipment. So, in the summer of 1949 we moved into the old "big house," the only move we have made in our fifty years of marriage.

It seemed huge to us. Its large white-frame design with peaked sections of roof was nothing like our cozy brick home, but we knew the big house would lend itself to wheelchairs or whatever else might be needed to care for a handicapped child. Besides, there was an elevator.

We made some changes, removing the large porte-cochere at the front entrance, adding a porch at one end overlooking the garden and a terrace which extended into the walled garden off the dining room.

Two small bedrooms, a hallway, and a bathroom at the head of the stairway made an ideal suite for Verlinda and Margaret. We had Verlinda's bathtub raised to a height which made it easier for us to lift her in and out and had a long counter built along the opposite wall to use as a changing table.

Our life was different in many other ways, too, ways that seem too unimportant to mention. Such a simple thing as taking family pictures became difficult to do. For a while I hated cards sent from our friends at Christmas—cards with pictures of lovely family gatherings of healthy, normal children.

There were no spur-of-the-moment excursions. It was necessary to make plans ahead of time before going anywhere so that someone would be in the house to care for Verlinda. When the children were small, this didn't seem too unusual, but later when they were older and Verlinda was the only "baby," it became more apparent.

Margaret was my great support during those years. We weathered people's negative attitudes together. Because of her, I could devote more time to working with the handicapped and retarded. Although I loved the times with Verlinda when Margaret was on vacation or on her days off, I know I did not have the emotional strength to care for Verlinda day in and day out without her help.

Caring for Verlinda brought out my creativity. I used an outboard-motor carrier to invent a lightweight chair on wheels that we could use instead of her heavy wheelchair. The brace man at the Watson Home, where Verlinda went for therapy, created a canvas seat and backrest for the carrier. It was marvelous! It was light and yet sturdy enough to survive rough roads and being tossed in and out of the car throughout the years.

I always felt disloyal when the rest of the family went off on a trip and Verlinda stayed home with Margaret. It never seemed quite fair to leave her behind just because she didn't fit into the normal world. In those days severely retarded people attracted more unkind attention than they do now because most were kept out of sight. In 1981, The Year of the Disabled brought about changes in the public's awareness, attitudes, and understanding. But there is still a long way to go before the prejudice and discrimination which cause difficulties for the mentally retarded are broken down.

We need to make a commitment to reach people through education regarding the mentally disabled, to open the Door marked "Retardation," so that others may realize there is nothing to be afraid of on the other side.

The world of the retarded can be very much like the kingdom of heaven if we see these people from God's perspective.

When we put them and ourselves in his hands, our values begin to change, and our lives begin to show the fruits of the Spirit. We begin to see the importance of seeking the gifts of love, joy, peace, patience, kindness, goodness, faithfulness, gentleness, and self-control mentioned in Galatians 5:22 and 23.

For myself, the opening of the Door brought blessing. Nancy emphasized one of many blessings when she said, "There are so many people we would never have known if it hadn't been for Dolly." Our experience was like that of dropping a pebble in the water, the ripples going on and on, always widening the circle. There are those who know and love the Lord who may or may not have an association with the handicapped but who care about the "least." There are those who work with the handicapped who may or may not know the Lord but who serve him nevertheless through their service and care of his family. And there are the disabled themselves and the members of their families.

It is a rich variety of people that cuts across race, religion, age, or social distinctions. I became a member of the whole human race and no longer felt enclosed in a small segment of it.

The sacrifice was Verlinda's—my child of grace. Without her my life would have continued to be narrow. I would have known about the people out there who were retarded, who suffered, who were discriminated against, but I would not have had the privilege of knowing them on a deep and personal level.

That is the great blessing on the other side of the Door. To experience the heartache of having a child who is different and then have that heartache grow into a beautiful service to God is nothing less than a miracle. It is like the mustard seed Jesus spoke about which "when it is sown it grows up and becomes the greatest of all shrubs, and puts forth large branches, so that the birds of the air can make nests in its shade" (Mark 4:31). Jesus was speaking about the kingdom of God.

Here is my meditation and song of praise:

> Lord, I walked through one Door when Verlinda was born, a Door that led into a room of grief. There was no turning back; the Door back to where I had been was closed and locked forever. I saw another Door, dimly at first, but it drew me. I opened it, or rather it opened for me, and I was invited to walk through. That was Jesus, the Door of my salvation.
>
> O, God, how I love that Door! Thank you for opening it, for allowing my eyes to behold Your glory. Jesus, I have entered the sheepfold by the Door, and you are my shepherd. Praise God from whom all blessings flow!

# 11
# Two Strands

*In all thy ways acknowledge him,
and he shall direct thy paths.*
PROVERBS 3:6, KJV

Verlinda brought two strands of change into my life. One strand emerged shortly after I crossed the threshold of the Door—the new dimension of the love of God and a relationship to Jesus Christ. This strand expanded my knowledge of the Bible and of people who shared a longing to help others through prayer and faith in the healing power of Jesus Christ.

The prayer fellowship begun by Bishop Pardue became the focal point and pattern of my life, and it continued for about ten years until the second strand—the strand involving my work with the handicapped—began.

Verlinda was about six years old when we took her to the D. T. Watson Home for Crippled Children to see Dr. Jessie Wright, an orthopedic doctor known around the world for her work in infantile paralysis. At that time most of the children living at the Home had had polio. There were also some children with other orthopedic problems such as osteomylitis, arthritis, and a few who were victims of cerebral palsy. The Home had an excellent school program and was equipped to serve the disabled child of average intelligence, not the retarded.

The Watson Home, now the D. T. Watson Rehabilitation Hospital, is located seventeen miles west of Pittsburgh, about five miles from our home. Since 1920 the lovely red-brick structure on seventy-five acres of lawns and wooded areas was literally "home" to many of the children who spent their growing-up years there. Their educational needs were met from nursery school through high school, and they received the necessary therapies: physical, occupational, speech, and training in the activities of daily living.

It was 1952 when we took Verlinda to see Dr. Wright. We didn't receive anything more favorable in the way of a prognosis, but she did prescribe a full body brace for Verlinda which would make it possible for her to sit more comfortably and even to stand. She also told us that the brace would help to prevent deformities. At first the brace seemed cruel to us, but as time passed we could see its benefits not only for Verlinda but also for those of us who cared for her. Instead of having to carry her and lift her from one place to another we could stand her on her feet and "walk" her.

Dr. Wright suggested that the speech pathologist see Verlinda to determine whether or not she had any hearing. I remember very well the day we took Verlinda to see Anne Gray, the director of speech and hearing at the Home. She was the first professional person we had seen who suggested that Verlinda might be capable of learning something and that she would like to work with her. Her philosophy, based on her faith in God, was that no child can be considered hopeless until given a chance to learn. She obviously loved the children with whom she worked.

Anne Gray was blessed with a very outgoing personality, and the children responded to her warmth and enthusiasm. There was an expectancy in her manner that almost demanded a response as she encouraged the children to vocalize and make specific sounds.

Margaret and I could see, when we watched her with Verlinda, that she was not in the least discouraged. She felt that Verlinda had some sight, and also that with the stimulation of listening to music and speech sounds with amplification through earphones, her attention to sound could be enhanced.

Anne saw Verlinda as a challenge. She was creative in her work; if one technique didn't bring a response, she would try something else. Soon she had Margaret and me thinking of ways we could try to reach Verlinda at home.

It wasn't long before I discovered that Anne Gray shared my concern about the lack of programs for children like Verlinda, the severely disabled. By that time I knew of other families who had been confronted with the same difficulties and disappointments that Henry and I had experienced in trying to find help.

During the war years I worked as a Red Cross nurse's aide in the hospital nursery with Adeline, the nurse in charge. One day, a few years after the war, we met while shopping in the village. Her little boy was with her, and it was apparent that he was developmentally delayed. I asked her about him. "It was the Rh-factor," she explained. I told her about Verlinda and all that we had been through with her, and then about Nancy and the exchange transfusion.

Then she said, "We have a little girl, too."

"Did she have the transfusion?" I asked.

Her answer was cause for sorrow and anger because the doctors, even knowing that Adeline was Rh-negative and that her first child already had problems, had not transfused the second baby. As a result, their little girl was severely handicapped with cerebral palsy.

I also knew Andrew Hanzel. I met his mother, Theo, through the prayer group at St. Stephen's. She was an English war-bride and had four children. One day I received a call from a mutual friend who said that the Hanzels had received some very bad news about their baby. "Would you go and see Theo?" she asked. "She needs to talk to someone."

I went that afternoon. Theo was as shattered as I had been. She was still in a state of shock and felt she was living a nightmare. Andrew had seemed normal for the first few months of his life. Then, at six months old, he stopped progressing. The doctor, a general practitioner who cared for their family, didn't seem to notice the delayed development, and so Theo tried to ignore it, too.

When Andrew was eleven months old she took him to a pediatrician who immediately saw that something was seriously wrong and placed Andrew in the Children's Hospital to be examined.

There his parents learned that Andrew had phenylketonuria (or PKU as it is better known). This is a rare metabolic disease which occurs when both father and mother have a missing gene. The missing gene contains the enzyme needed for digesting phenylanaline, a chemical in all protein foods. If the problem is discovered within the first three weeks of life, a protein-free diet can be substituted for the infant. If not, the brain damage which occurs is irreversible.

Andrew's brain had already been damaged by the unassimilated protein in milk and other foods. The doctor told the Hanzels that nothing could be done. "Take him home and give him lots of tender loving care," was all the doctor said. "This child will probably never walk or talk and probably will never know you. You will eventually have to institutionalize him."

I listened to her story, and we shared our experiences of shock, fear, and grief. Together we were comforted. Neither one of us had ever heard of PKU. I looked at Andrew as he lay in his crib. A beautiful, blond, blue-eyed baby, he looked far more normal than Verlinda had looked, and it was hard to believe that he couldn't do anything but lie in his crib.

A long and difficult road lay ahead for Theo. Andrew was put on the special diet in the hope that it was not too late and that further brain damage might be prevented. But it *was* too late, the damage was done, and Andrew lived out his life like Verlinda, unable to do anything for himself—completely dependent upon others for his care.

I stopped in to see Theo several times during that week, and as we talked and watched the helplessness of Andrew, I knew that he was a candidate for some kind of help at the Watson Home and looked forward to Anne Gray seeing him. I knew she would do her best to reach Andrew. This experience with Andrew increased our desire to get a program started for these children who were seen by everyone as untrainable and useless.

Henry and I had searched for such programs when Verlinda was younger. There were no St. Peter's Child Development Centers, preschools for the developmentally delayed, nothing to advise parents about how to feed their children or suggest toys that would encourage response and coordination.

Parents tried on their own but soon became discouraged. "What's the use?" they would ask. "It's too discouraging. She'll never learn anything. The doctor was right." And they often gave up. It was too difficult to overcome the pervasive negative attitude regarding anything to do with the retarded or physically handicapped.

Most professionals thought it was a waste of time to try to teach or train the lowest of the low. Anne Gray's colleagues laughed at her for taking on a child like Verlinda, and they were rather contemptuous of me for taking Verlinda to the Home for therapy. The attitude was, "What on earth does this mother think she's going to do with this child who is almost blind, almost deaf, and who is totally incapacitated by physical limitations?"

But Anne and I continued to discuss the need to give these children a chance. We knew that the regular program of the Watson Home was geared to higher functioning children and were aware of the attitude of the staff, so we discussed other ways we might meet the needs of the children and their families.

Finally we went to Dr. Wright and the administrator of the Home at that time. They did not want to bring the children into the program because no one was experienced in working with them. It was untilled ground.

After several meetings we settled on a weekend program, a trial to see if the children could benefit in any way. We were thrilled! In January of 1955 this pilot program, enthusiastically underwritten by Henry, took off. This class for six nonambulatory, severely handicapped children all under nine years of age got started. They gathered at the Home each weekend for therapy and training from that time until June.

The staff consisted of a physical therapist, an occupational therapist, Anne, the speech therapist, a school teacher, and two practical nurses. These people were willing to give up their weekends to help the children and their parents. I am forever grateful to them. From nine in the morning to four in the afternoon each Saturday and Sunday, the children received full treatment, testing, and training.

The program was completely experimental since the staff had no idea which methods would produce results. But at the end of the six-month trial period, the administration decided that the children would be admitted to the regular program at the Home. Not only had the six little ones made enough progress to prove to the administration that it was worthwhile to work with them, but they had endeared themselves to the staff!

The weekend program introduced me to the delight and rewards of working with these little ones and drew me out of my overinvestment in Verlinda. We prayed for them and loved them, and when one of them learned something new, we all rejoiced together. I remember our excitement when Verlinda tried to say, "Apple," while looking at a bright picture of an apple!

Shortly after the close of the weekend program, Theo Hanzel

and her four children moved from Sewickley to another suburb on the other side of Pittsburgh. Theo admits that they were running away to a place where nobody knew them, a place where they could hide.

Although Andrew's grandparents lived in the community to which they moved, Andrew's grandfather never knew that his grandson was retarded. The secret was kept from him for fear of bringing on a heart attack.

Andrew continued to come to the Watson Home for therapy once a week. He lived with his family until he was about eleven years old when Theo, who was barely five feet tall, could no longer carry him.

Theo is a remarkable woman—one of the most courageous people I have ever known. With four children, one of them totally dependent, she had her hands full. There was no "Margie" there to help, no family to share the burden, and yet she managed to be mother to the four, remained active in church, took night courses to obtain a degree, learned to drive a car so she could bring Andrew to the Home for his therapy, and generally kept going at a pace that would daunt the hardiest. I have never ceased to wonder at her.

Finally Andrew was admitted to Western Center, a large state institution, and Theo obtained work there as an aide in a unit housing forty adolescent boys.

The weekend program at the Watson Home led me into working with the handicapped almost full-time as a volunteer for many years. One day in 1962 Anne Gray and I were invited to assist in another program for retarded preschool children. At first we were asked to come one day per week to do some testing in a small school housed in the St. Peter's Episcopal Church in Brentwood on the far side of Pittsburgh. Since then the program and my involvement steadily expanded. There are now six of these centers in the county serving up to twenty-four preschool children in each center.

St. Peter's program is unusual in its work with parents. Anne

Gray and I were actively involved in the parents' meetings for some time. We found families struggling with discouraging and sometimes insurmountable problems. One single mother whose twin boys were in one of the centers worked as an entertainer to support them. Another family had seven children, three of whom were currently enrolled in St. Peter's. The parents were both retarded.

One mother had fallen downstairs with her seven-month-old baby in her arms. As a result he was blind and severely brain damaged, an infant like Verlinda.

I shared some of the pain these parents experienced. Many were discriminated against in their neighborhoods. Parents of retarded children belong to a minority group and can expect the same prejudice and discrimination that other minority groups receive from people who act out of fear rather than through faith and love. Keeping this in mind helps us not to be so hurt by the lack of understanding we sometimes experience from others. These experiences promote better identification with other minority groups who suffer the hurts by virtue of their color, race, or sex. God wants to work through parents, expressing his love to "all sorts and conditions of men," especially those in bodies that are considered unlovable by many.

The St. Peter's program represents for me one of the greatest blessings brought into my life by Verlinda. Because it was originally staffed by volunteers, I felt no lack of professional status. Each person involved in the program respected the others.

One year during my heaviest involvement at St. Peter's, the director of the centers sent my name to the Allegheny County Bar Association as a candidate for the Liberty Bell Award given annually to a "nonlawyer who has made an outstanding contribution to some civic or humanitarian activity." I was selected to receive it for my service in the field of working with handicapped children. What an honor and privilege!

This branching out beyond my life with Verlinda to the program

*Two Strands*

at Watson Home in Sewickley and later to my contributions through the St. Peter's Centers represents the second strand of my life. There were times when I missed the focus of the prayer group, but I have never regretted my active participation in the lives of the children with whom I worked. To me it was a calling and a ministry, and while some others saw me unnecessarily "putting all my eggs in one basket," I saw myself serving God with real purpose.

# 12
# A Day in the Life of Verlinda

*Truly, I say to you,
as you did it to one of the least of these
my brethren, you did it to me.*
MATTHEW 25:40

As Verlinda grew older and we became more accustomed to caring for her, her life took on a scheduled routine. We seldom broke from the pattern that evolved from her needs and the family structure. Unless she had had a sleepless and restless night, she was awakened at 6:30 or 7:00 o'clock in the morning. Since she spent the night face down, we turned her over onto her back and removed her night splints. These splints were light-weight leg braces with open-toed shoes attached. They had a bar about eighteen inches long between the shoes which kept her legs in good alignment and prevented deformities and contractures from developing during the night. She lay with her toes over the edge of the mattress with sandbags on either side of her body.

Freed from her splints, she could stretch and move her legs about and respond to our touch. She communicated with either sounds of pleasure or of pain and distress. Then she was bathed and dressed (dressing included a hearing aid, her glasses, and a full body brace), and placed in a small, armless Victorian chair to have her breakfast. We put a wide leather strap around her rib cage and the back of the chair to help her maintain her balance, and a "head piece" was inserted into the top of the back brace to hold her head in place, keeping her chin down, and thus putting her head in proper position for swallowing. Verlinda had a tendency to throw her head back, and so it took force to keep it forward.

The body brace was the kind required for support by many children and adults afflicted with cerebral palsy or other paralyzing conditions. Verlinda's brace was quite heavy. It was made of steel, and the parts which came in contact with her body were covered with soft leather or a smooth plastic molded around the steel. A canvas corset with leather straps buckled in the front and supported her chest and abdomen. It was attached to the steel supports in the back and was boned like a corset.

Straps with felt padding came over the shoulders and buckled on to the canvas corset. Bands of plastic that attached to the leg braces buckled to encircle her thighs; knee pads of leather and felt were also attached to the steel leg braces and buckled at the sides of her knees.

The leg braces consisted of steel bars that went down each side of the leg at the bottom of which were two holes. On each side of her shoes were steel bars which were made with two protrusions to fit into the holes. It took strength to force the protrusions, which were like little knobs, into the holes. When Verlinda was rigid and spastic it was especially difficult.

Once into her brace it was possible to stand Verlinda on her feet and "walk" her to her chair. The brace weighed about twenty pounds. So, although it was possible to lift her in it, it was sometimes awkward to carry her, and it proved easier to stand her up when possible and swing her legs forward by shifting her weight from one side to the other.

Lockable joints at the knees and hips could be unlocked, allowing her to sit. But if we were having a problem with Verlinda's spasticity, it was difficult to lock or unlock these joints.

Verlinda's breakfast consisted of fruit juice, cereal and banana flakes, pureed fruit, and a glass of milk. We encouraged her to drink through a straw. Her tongue was often very active, so it was difficult for her to drink from a cup.

Verlinda liked to blow through the straw so we used a reverse-valve device invented by Anne Gray. The blo-blok was placed on the end of the straw. When the child sucked, the valve opened, but if the child blew into the straw, the valve closed—preventing bubble-blowing and the accompanying mess.

In the development of speech patterns, it is important for a child to learn to suck before he or she blows. Therefore, although the children were denied the pleasure of bubble blowing, the blo-blok strengthened the tongue and throat muscles needed for speech development. Strangely enough, Verlinda was the only child we ever saw who was able to make bubbles in spite of the blo-blok, a mystery we never solved.

Verlinda's tongue activity made it difficult to get food into her mouth and down her throat. Sometimes it took more than an hour to feed her.

Once she finished her breakfast, she was moved from her chair to the "potty" chair, a movable commode on wheels. There was always a certain amount of tension at this time because when Verlinda's elimination became irregular, she ran the risk of having a seizure or of being very spastic and uncomfortable for the rest of the day.

At least three mornings a week Verlinda went to the Watson

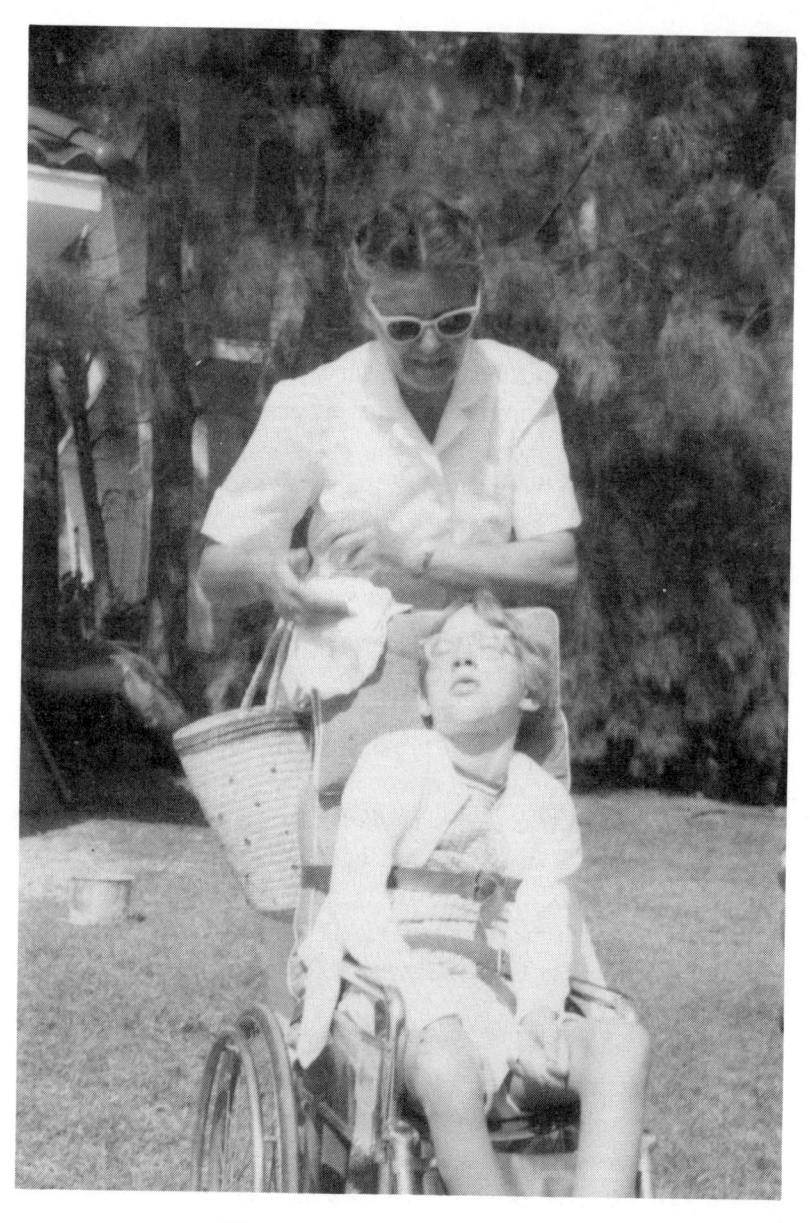

*Nancy and eight-year-old Verlinda*

# A Day in the Life of Verlinda

Home for therapy, so when all the morning preparations were finished, we put her in her canvas chair on wheels, rolled her down the ramp into the garage, lifted her into the car, put the chair in the back of the car, and were off. It was generally about nine o'clock by this time.

Verlinda received physical therapy for many years at the Home. She was a favorite among the staff, who always seemed glad to see "Dolly" and made a big fuss over her, as did the other children.

She was also part of a group of nonverbal children with whom Anne Gray worked. As the years went by, many of those other little ones developed speech, but there were always new ones coming in with whom Verlinda could join. This group was given exercises on the basic skills of chewing, sucking, and swallowing. Lots of music accompanied hand-clapping, foot-tapping, and raising the arms up and down, etc. The children banged on drums and jingled bells to develop rhythm patterns. The session was always completed with a "peanut-butter lollipop." Each child was given a tongue depressor with peanut butter on one end. The child had to press his lips together over the peanut butter to pull it off. This technique was designed to improve lip closure, but to the children it was the treat of the day.

Margaret generally stayed with Verlinda through the morning activities and lunch, and then she and Verlinda were taken home while I stayed on to continue my work with some of the other children. Back at home, Verlinda had an afternoon nap, and then Margaret and she went for a long walk, always accompanied by the dogs and sometimes the cat.

Margaret (our Mary Poppins with her snapping brown eyes, thick dark hair, and red cheeks) loved those walks and pushed Verlinda in her wheelchair up and down the farm roads. I still see her in my mind's eye walking very briskly, her back as straight as though a ramrod had been put there instead of a spine. She and Verlinda were out in all kinds of weather.

After her walk, Verlinda listened to music. Whether Verlinda could make anything of what she heard or saw, we did not know. Tests suggested that she had some sight and hearing, though both were severely impaired. She had a hearing aid and glasses in the hope that some signals would get through and her brain would be stimulated to make some interpretation.

Sometimes she listened to the music while lying on her bed, sometimes sitting in her chair, but usually we put her in her "standing table." This contraption was shaped like an L. There was a platform on which she stood and a backboard with slots in it through which a restraining strap could be put to hold her in place. There were other holes in which arms of a tray attached. We'd place her toys, blocks, a bell, or a drum on the tray.

Verlinda was required to spend a certain amount of time each day in the standing table. Being on her feet improved her circulation. We worked with her there every afternoon and also in the mornings when she didn't go to the Home. Working with her consisted of getting her to hold objects or reach for a bright toy or ball or to track an object or light held at eye level.

There were times when Verlinda would be too fussy to do any of these activities. Then we took her out of her braces and just held and rocked her in the rocking chair, listened to music, or sang to her. In the summer months Verlinda enjoyed "swimming" in our pool as she lay supported by an innertube, moving her legs and squealing with delight when the other children splashed her.

Sometimes my mother came and took Verlinda for a drive. My mother loved Verlinda. She would sit by her side, holding her hand and talking to her lovingly. It was hard for her to be reconciled to the braces because she thought they must be uncomfortable for Verlinda.

Verlinda had supper about 5:30. A small refrigerator in her room kept a supply of pureed foods, juices, and milk in it. Again the speed

# A Day in the Life of Verlinda

of the meal depended on her tongue, but usually by 6:30 she was finished, and it was time to reverse the morning process of removing her clothes and the braces. Most evenings we gave her a whirlpool bath which was relaxing and good for the circulation. Verlinda appeared to enjoy it and generally made very happy sounds while she was in it. I'm sure that after having been in those heavy braces all day, it was a blessed relief to feel the water swirling around her.

Out of the tub she was dried and powdered, dressed in a pretty nightgown, strapped into her night splints, and once again placed face down on the bed with her toes over the end of the mattress;

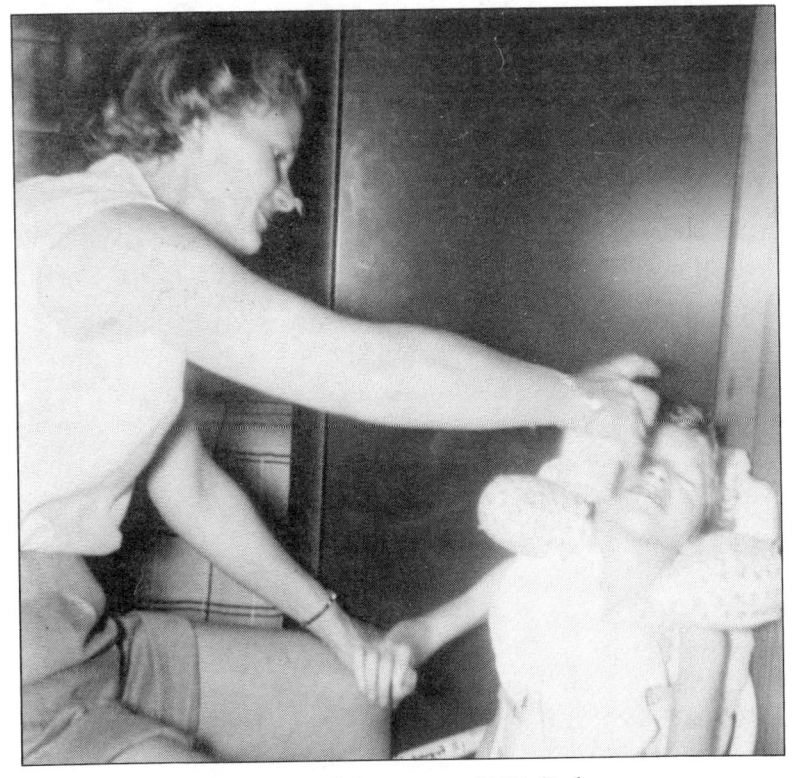

*Nancy and eleven-year-old Verlinda*

and finally, the two heavy sandbags were placed on either side of her body.

When Margaret was out for the day, her monthly weekend, or her month's vacation, I continued the routine pretty much the same but with much less efficiency. There were other demands that had to be incorporated, activities with the other children, telephone calls, etc. There was no way I could carry on the way Margaret did, nor did I want to. I enjoyed being more relaxed in caring for Verlinda. But there were times, too, when nothing seemed to go right, and the feelings of pressure built up.

Sometimes my friend, Eleanor Nevin, would come at suppertime with a custard for Dolly. Eventually she earned the name "Aunt Custard." She held Verlinda's hand while I fed her, and we would pray together as Verlinda was settled for the night.

Eleanor saw Verlinda as her child of grace, too—the instrument God used to bring her closer to him. When her husband had a heart attack and was ill for some time before his death, she felt comforted and sustained throughout that difficult time by the support of our prayer group. In turn, she was a wonderful support to me. I knew that she loved "Dolly" as she was, and I could share my feelings and pray with her when the going got rough.

It helped when she came to visit Verlinda at suppertime. Sometimes it had been a bad day, and I was finding it hard to be patient. It was difficult, at times, to love a child who wasn't toilet-trained and never would be, who spat more food out of her mouth than she swallowed and always would. There were times when it would suddenly seem too much for me. I felt trapped by a situation that appeared to have no end. I often wanted to fall apart, to feel sorry for myself. At such times I was lost until I prayed my way back to the knowledge that I was serving God through doing these familiar acts of washing, clothing, bracing, and feeding Verlinda, and that it was a privilege to serve him in this way because I was ministering to the least of his children. With my vision refocused, my courage would return, and once again I would be lifted to a place of love.

Sometimes God restores us directly by filling us with peace and strength, and sometimes he works through someone else who listens to us with empathy and understanding until the tension leaves us and we are able to see things from his perspective. Eleanor was one of those people in my life.

Jesus Christ took a basin and washed the feet of his disciples to teach them humility and to show them that without serving one another in this lowly way, they could have no part in him. He said, "If I then, your Lord and Teacher, have washed your feet, you also ought to wash one another's feet. For I have given you an example, that you should do as I have done for you" (John 13:14-15).

In one sense my handicapped child *was* Christ, and whatever I did for Verlinda, I did it for him. As long as I held this vision in my mind and heart, there was no task too difficult to perform. What wouldn't I do for my Jesus? It was only when I forgot it or even didn't want to think about it that things became impossible to do one more time.

We have to pray for the humility we need to perform such duties for others, whether it is our own children or some other person we are responsible for in our work or in our family. We need the humility Jesus had when he took the towel and washed his disciples' feet.

Verlinda was a fragment that we gathered up. While we cared for her and brought daily nourishment to her, filling all her needs, she also nourished us. Without her I would not have been fed. She led me to the "living water" Jesus promised the Samaritan woman at the well (John 4:10). She led me to the Door of the world of faith.

# 13
# Unseen Things

*We look not to the things that are seen
but to the things that are unseen;
for the things that are seen are transient,
but the things that are unseen are eternal.*
2 CORINTHIANS 4:18

One day while I was working at the Watson Home, the thought came to me that we who are considered normal could learn from the children with whom we worked.

When our prayer group at St. Stephen's first started praying for Verlinda and other handicapped children, our intense desire was to bring about a change in them that would make them like us, better equipped mentally and physically for the normal world. Of course, this was also the goal of the work we were engaged in at the Watson Home. We wanted the children to develop skills and abilities that would help them gain some independence. I grieved over their necessity always to have someone else care for their most personal needs.

"It would be bad enough," I thought, "never to be able to reach for something to eat if I was hungry, or to get a glass of water if I was thirsty, but how awful it would be to have another person take me to the bathroom, comb my hair, and do every other personal thing for me."

But that day I realized that instead of trying to *make them more like us*, there are ways in which *we should become more like them.* They have qualities that every follower of Jesus Christ wants to attain. Often they demonstrate the fruits of the spirit in their patience, faith, and meekness. Their joy and sense of humor in the face of their limitations is sometimes awesome. They have an inner strength that is proof to me that they are close to God. I believe they act as leaven in the normal population, bringing us into a closer relationship to God.

Verlinda was the leaven in our family. Because of her needs we were called to pray, and in praying we developed a spiritual life.

Because communication on the conscious level with Verlinda was limited, we began to understand the importance of the unconscious. I began to think and meditate on Verlinda's spiritual side. I thought of the similarity between her and other creations of God in nature, such as flowers or trees. So much is hidden about this aspect of God's creation. Consider the seed or acorn or tulip bulb or crocus. Who would dream of the beauty that lies within these strange looking forms? Who could imagine the beauty of the oak tree hidden within an acorn or believe that something so large could grow out of something so small? It takes a childlike faith to look at an acorn and accept the fact that all the potential for an oak tree lies within.

As I meditated on these things and praised God for those things that are hidden from us, I was released from the outer and physical appearance of Verlinda. I came to think of her as an inner being growing from within even though I didn't see any outward evidence. I couldn't imagine what would unfold from within any more than I could imagine the beauty of the tulip unfolding from that strange looking brown bulb. I believe that if we pray for the inner life of these children to develop, we will see the branches of their lives reaching out in beauty and giving shade to others like the branches of a tree.

Each of us has an inner life, of course, but all too often we are so busy with outer cares that we don't take time to nurture it. It is important to minister to and nurture the inner life in our handicapped children, through prayer and faith and love, for when we do, it unfolds in God's creativity.

Father John Banks encouraged this approach. He asked that Henry, Margaret, and I pray each night by Verlinda's crib. He said to us, "It is not necessary to beg God for anything: 'Your Heavenly Father knoweth what things ye have need of, before ye ask Him' (Matthew 6:8). But it *is* necessary to surround her with united prayer, love, and thanksgiving. This will prove irresistible; it will penetrate into her deeper soul, her subconscious, and make her able to receive healing by a coordination of nerve, mind, and muscle. Before long," he added, "some big obstacle will yield to this barrage of love and prayer and faith. Or through this persevering prayer, the doctors may find some more effective way of helping her."

I began to think about the unconscious or subconscious mind. It has been compared to the section of an iceberg that lies beneath the surface of the water. This unconscious part of us contains greater strength than we can possibly imagine with our conscious minds, a strength that enables us to do things in an emergency that we could never do otherwise. The tremendous power that lies within us is seldom realized.

I believe that we should consider this unconscious area in our handicapped children. They, too, have come into the world with this great and mysterious potential; it is a common denominator in all of us.

Paul said, "Each one has his own special gift from God" (1 Corinthians 7:7). How does this apply to each handicapped child we know? With those as profoundly handicapped as Verlinda, the common categories of overt gifts don't seem to apply. Therefore their gifts must be those of the heart and spirit. This was true for Verlinda. God gave her his power, love, and mercy in unusually creative ways.

Verlinda responded to prayer. It was particularly noticeable when Sam Odom, the Associate Rector at St. Stephen's, would come to see her. A Virginian with a pleasant southern drawl, Sam was a very loving and gentle man who came faithfully almost every week to pray for Verlinda. Sometimes she was fussy, and we knew that she had discomfort of some kind. Sam would stand there talking to Margaret and me for awhile in his rich, tonal voice, and Verlinda would gradually become quieter.

Then he would put his hand on her head and begin to pray. Verlinda would immediately start to vocalize in her way of expressing joy: "O-o-oh, oh-ah, buh, buh, buh, bo-bo." She waved her arms about and squealed. It was amazing and delightful to see the change in her. We knew that something we couldn't understand had taken place. It was a loving time for all of us, the sort of experience that Father John had prescribed. The room was filled with God's love when Sam came to visit. Verlinda obviously felt this, and we knew that she had received a blessing through the unseen channels of her unconscious, her spirit, the part of her that was made in the image and likeness of God.

# 14

# Was It Worth It?

*Gather up the fragments left over,
that nothing may be lost.*
JOHN 6:12

After the feeding of the five thousand, Christ told the disciples to gather up the fragments of extra food so that nothing would be lost. Do you remember how he fed that multitude? The situation looked pretty hopeless. They had nothing but a few loaves and fishes, not more than enough for a boy's lunch. But our Lord was able to take what little was available and do something with it, in spite of all the doubts and lack of faith the disciples may have felt.

During the years that I worked at the Watson Home, many parents brought their children in once a week for speech therapy. Some were severely retarded and had never received any training or therapy. Anne Gray's reputation for giving handicapped youngsters a chance was increasing. Anne truly loved the "least." She never gave up on them and was an encourager to many parents. I frequently heard her say to them, "I don't know how far he'll go, but we won't know 'til we try."

There was one little boy who came to us when he was nine years old. E.J. was rather an odd looking little fellow with wide open, slightly bulging eyes, and large, protruding upper teeth. He had no speech or any other skills although he could walk.

His parents had been told that E.J. would never learn anything, and so for nine years they did not try to teach him. He was not toilet trained or able to feed himself. In fact, he was still eating baby food and drinking from a bottle. To look at him, you'd think he was a child only a mother could love, but all of us in the speech department fell in love with E.J. and looked forward eagerly to his weekly appointment. We soon found that even though he couldn't talk, he communicated on a nonverbal level in a most engaging way.

As E.J. began to respond in the program, his mother became a new person. She and his father were thrilled to know that they could expect something from their son, that they could discipline him. For the first time in his life they took him out without feeling ashamed or embarrassed. They learned that they could love him in a more normal way because they saw others loving him and recognizing him as a person.

There was another little girl about three or four years old who came to Anne for therapy. She had no speech and lay limply in her mother's arms. Her parents shared the same, familiar story of having been told that their baby would never learn anything. The little girl looked uncared for, her clothes ragged and her hair dirty and uncombed.

But one day a few weeks later the parents arrived with a new light in their eyes. The father was carrying little Wendy, and when he gave her to Anne to hold, Anne saw that the child was wearing a clean and pretty dress. Her hair, shiny and brushed, was tied with a pink ribbon.

"What's happened?" Anne exclaimed. "Wendy looks beautiful! You have her all dressed up!"

The parents shared that they had not been able to love their baby. "We didn't know how," they said, "until we saw you loving her—and then we realized how lovable she is."

The change in E.J. and little Wendy and their parents points out the need for us to pray for God's love to flow through us to these children, not only for their sakes but also in order to dispel the fears of others and to change the attitude of many who see such children as queer and unlovable. When God's love works in us the seemingly unlovable become lovable.

Was it worthwhile to give Verlinda so much care and expend so much energy on her body? Is it worthwhile to work with any of the profoundly retarded and severely handicapped? Would it have been better if the doctors and nurses had not worked so hard to bring her through her first critical illness? Would it have been kinder and more humane for them not to have resuscitated her, given those transfusions, worked over her day and night those many weeks?

The same questions are raised today, and now parents have the added burden of making decisions about life support systems. In the case of a baby born with spina-bifida, parents must decide whether to operate or let the baby die. I thank God that Henry and I were not called upon to make such decisions during Verlinda's illness or at any time during her life.

A few years ago Joan, the daughter of friends of ours, had to make such a decision when her second child was born with spina-bifida, the incomplete development of the spine. She and her husband, Bill, decided on life for little Jennifer. But it was hard for the relatives to adjust to the trauma and heartbreak of the baby's condition. So at Joan's request, I wrote a letter explaining, from my experience, how a handicapped child can be a blessing. This is some of what I shared:

> [Handicapped children] bring a new dimension into people's lives. Most of us grow up and move about with people who are "normal"—people who look right and talk right and do all the right things, and we tend to be fearful of anybody who is different. However, being closely associated with a handicapped child, seeing her and others as babies and watching them grow and develop at their own rate, we come to know them as more normal than not. We see that they have feelings and personality qualities that make up a real person. They have the same needs we have: the need to be loved and accepted, the need to be teased and scolded, the need to express themselves. Being with them helps us see things in a new perspective and our values begin to change. We become more aware of people as individuals.
>
> You know how people rally and work together when something like a disaster—a fire or flood or whatever—comes along? Well, it's kind of like that. You share the common desire to make things better for the handicapped. You share a common bond which breaks through falseness and makes your life real and alive instead of just a busy existence.
>
> This is what life is all about. No matter how hard the struggle will be, the life of this family will have real meaning and they'll know many wonderful people. Being able to share empathetically the feelings of others is a tremendous blessing—and I don't limit this to the category of mental or physical handicaps. It carries over into all areas of suffering and all kinds of people who are discriminated against in some way.
>
> Having to lean on God every step of the way is probably the greatest blessing of all. When the physical world we live in is impaired in some way, then we look more deeply into the world of faith. It becomes more real to us—it is the great common

denominator—the part of all of us that can never be crippled or handicapped. It's the bridge that connects the world of the normal and the world of the handicapped.

Think of the world without a Helen Keller and the impossible things she accomplished. Who can tell right now what very special gift Jennifer may have for all of you who are close to her? Think of this when your heart feels like breaking.

Some time after reading my letters, Joan wrote these comments to me:

> We will never be able to express to you how much your thoughts meant to us. I feel so grateful to you for the positive slant of all your communications. Billy and I found that . . . when we had gotten over the shock of the situation and were trying hard to push forward with strong positive thoughts, most people were still pouring pity on us and expressing their sorrow at our tragedy. We found these attitudes very debilitating especially since we had lost any feeling that it was a "tragedy." We desperately needed someone to help us see the good.

Joan went on to describe Jennifer's condition, all the operations she would have to undergo and then she said,

> In looking at the whole picture there are lots of problems—she'll have many operations, but there is good, too. She has so much to work with, and she's an adorable, lovable little baby. It's impossible to feel sad. I'm discouraged at times, but she's far from tragic. I've already felt enriched from this new life with Jennifer.

I share these letters because they are proof that God works through situations that without him would be tragedies without any hope.

Jennifer is in her teens now. The years have not been easy for her and her family, but she has proved to be a great joy to them as she embraces life with a spirit and personality that are unimpaired. A lot of time and energy has been spent on her through the years, just as time and energy were spent on Verlinda and the other children we worked with, but we can be sure that we are following God's will when we choose to "gather up the fragments" and bring them to him to be blessed.

# 15
# Developing Talents

*Take the talent from him,
and give it to him who has the ten talents.*
MATTHEW 25:28

We are all familiar with the parable of the talents. As I grew more alert to the teachings of Christ I began to apply them to my own life. In this parable I learned that Christ does not want us to bury anything that we have received. If we do, we will be chastened. On the other hand, if we develop and increase that which we have received, more will be given to us.

It is easy to invest ourselves in the lives of our normal children. We watch them grow and develop and see the increase in their value as we give them opportunities for education and achievement. We invest in them, and they give us some return. They are worth struggling over because we can see the results and have visual proof that they have increased in value just as the man with the five talents could see his property doubled. We wouldn't consider doing anything else because the reward that we receive is so obvious.

But what about the man with only one talent? Even though his motive was a reasonable one—he wanted to be sure he did not lose the talent—he didn't do what was expected of him. He did nothing to bring about even a small increase. Therefore his talent was taken from him. God wants us to use everything we have and strive to get the greatest value from it.

Sometimes it didn't seem worth the struggle to keep investing in our "one talent" child. Certainly it would have been a great deal easier to stop searching for ways that might help her and just let her be comfortable and clean and cared for. So why did we keep on? After all, the progress we saw was so slight—an occasional turning of her head in response to a sound or an improvement in her ability to suck through a straw.

We kept on because we had gone beyond focusing on Verlinda's inabilities and were looking at what she *might* accomplish or in what ways the other children with whom we were working might benefit from our work with her.

During the time when the weekend program at the Watson Home was in progress, Anne Gray and I attended a seminar on cerebral palsy in Brooklyn. We were impressed with the presentation of Dr. Temple Fay, a neurosurgeon and psychiatrist from Philadelphia and former professor at Temple University Medical School. We introduced ourselves to him afterward and asked him if he would come to the Watson Home sometime.

Later on this remarkable man came to lecture to the staff and work with some of the patients. Anne and I were thrilled. We felt he was years ahead of his time with his innovative theories and techniques. He earnestly sought God's guidance and was constantly searching for answers to the problem of severe disabilities and for techniques that would help even the most handicapped.

When Henry and I took Verlinda to see him in Philadelphia, we were inspired by his positive attitude. "I'm tired of everyone looking at what isn't there," he said. "Let's look at what *is* there." He did not hold out any false hopes or unrealistic prognosis, but he gave us specific instructions to carry out. Once again we felt that we had something solid to go on in our day-to-day routine.

Dr. Fay asked us to have a pneumoencephalagram done on Verlinda while we were in Philadelphia. He reported the results: "Verlinda's brain looks like Swiss cheese." He knew there was very little to work with, but that didn't deter him from trying. "I can be honest with you," he told us, "Verlinda isn't going to get a college degree, but who knows how far we can take her otherwise. Maybe all she'll learn is how to get food from her plate to her mouth, but what an accomplishment that would be."

We went away from him with renewed confidence and encouragement. The future was not such an unknown quantity because we were working toward a goal. It seemed like we were freer to love Verlinda.

It was through one of his theories that Verlinda's convulsions were controlled. In a paper on his dehydration theory, Dr. Fay wrote, "According to the observations of Hippocrates, the brains of persons with epilepsy are 'unusually moist.'" So he developed a regime to limit Verlinda's fluid intake, thus reducing the amount of excess fluid on the brain which can occur when the mechanism that controls the disposition of liquids in the body is damaged. With this program Verlinda's seizures became less and less frequent and finally ceased altogether.

But Dr. Fay's neuromuscular reflex therapy played the biggest role in our lives. This therapy was based on the evolution of the central nervous system. He had studied the lower forms of life and felt that these patterns could be utilized to help retarded children perform at a higher level. The study of the development in a human infant shows the same progression of development. From this he developed basic movement patterns of crawling and creeping. For many years we exercised Verlinda and other children passively through these movement patterns. There were a few times when Verlinda was able to move on her own in a basic crawling movement, but we noted no significant change or progress in her from this therapy. Dr. Fay stressed that he was working for "purposeful movement from random activity."

In the winter of 1956, the Watson Home agreed to send some severely handicapped children to Florida to participate in a study Dr. Fay was conducting. We joined forces with him and rented an apartment on the beach near Sarasota. For several years Dr. Fay had dreamed of working with cerebral palsied children testing his theory of basic movement patterns in the sand and buoyant salt water. Some of his patients from other parts of the country and five children from the Watson Home took part in the program.

We flew south one cold morning in February. Henry procured the company plane, and we filled it with the children, a nurse, and physical therapist from the Watson Home, and Verlinda, Margaret, Henry, and myself. The excitement and anticipation were tremendous.

Henry was unable to stay, but since Verlinda was one of the children included in the program, Margaret and I stayed on. Anne Gray joined us later, and her dream of working closely with Dr. Fay was realized.

I had the opportunity of working not only with Verlinda but with the other children as well. I appreciated Dr. Fay's great respect for mothers. His attitude increased my self-esteem, and for the first time in my adult life, I didn't resent my lack of a college degree.

The warm weather and Florida sunshine was a wonderful respite for all of us from the wintry north, although we worked hard all day putting the children through the techniques Dr. Fay was teaching.

We spent long hours in a kneeling position on the sand as the children attempted the homolateral and contralateral crawling and creeping movements. Sometimes five of us stood in the shallow water, each one holding on to one part of a child: one on the right arm, one on the left, the same with the legs and one holding the head and turning it from side to side as the arms and legs were moved up and down through the reflex patterns. Sometimes we piled sand all around the children with only their heads exposed so they could feel what it was like to be quiet and free of the continual random activity of their arms and legs.

A framework was erected on the sand. It had a bar across the top from which hung a sling. The children were put upright in the sling with their feet touching the sand, so the rough surface of the sand could stimulate the nerves in their feet, making them aware of their feet in relation to the rest of their bodies.

In the evening we took Verlinda for drives and often picnicked on the beach. Dr. Fay was an excellent cook and made gourmet barbecued seafood.

Patty was one of the children with whom Dr. Fay assigned me to work. She was a beautiful, four-year-old girl with sparkling black eyes and short black curls. Because they had several children before Patty, her parents suspected something was wrong when she didn't sit up at six months or hold her head up with any degree of stability. Until then she had seemed normal because of the brightness of her face and her normal response to communication.

When Patty was eight months old her parents took her to Children's Hospital in Boston where she was diagnosed as having cerebral palsy. They were told to take her home and love her while she was a baby and when she was older to put her in an institution. No suggestion of therapy or training was given. Once again a family fell back on its own resources and searched for help. Fortunately this family found Dr. Fay.

Patty presently works in a sheltered workshop—not an ideal situation for a person of her intelligence, but again there is nothing else available. She lives in an apartment house where other disabled people live and where aides are provided to help all of them with their daily needs. Her family is very active in organizations for the disabled. Through the years they have been tireless in their efforts to help Patty reach her full potential and have been rewarded by seeing her achieve a remarkable independence. Though her speech is handicapped, her mental ability to communicate has never been limited, and she portrays an inspiring example of perseverance and patience in making herself understood, even to the point of spelling each word letter by letter until the listener grasps the meaning.

Patty stayed at the Watson Home several times during her early years. I worked with her there, and we became close friends. Since her home and family were so far away, she came to stay with us sometimes for weekends. Recently Patty came for a week's visit with us. It was lovely to see her again, to share the gospel with her, and to have her receive Jesus Christ as Lord and Savior.

Our involvement with Dr. Fay continued until the time of his death in 1963. We miss his inspiration but have never ceased to draw on the vast store of knowledge we gained during the years of our association with him. Verlinda stayed two or three times at his Rehabilitation Center for six weeks of concentrated therapy. Margaret and I took turns caring for her there and always benefitted from our stay.

Jesus said to those who doubled their talents, "Well done, good and faithful servant; you have been faithful over a little, I will set you over much; enter into the joy of your master" (Matthew 25:21). In other words, "Share with me in the joy that comes from using the gifts that I entrusted to you."

God judges us not by our successes but by our endeavors and by our faithfulness. His standards are not our standards. We are not asked to do the impossible, but we *are* asked and expected to do what we can. The poet and preacher, Edward Hale, wrote:

> I am only one,
> But still I am one.
> I cannot do everything,
> But still I can do something;
> And because I cannot do everything
> I will not refuse to do the something that I can do.

Verlinda's condition could have been a buried talent and probably would have been had I not met Jesus Christ and made the decision to follow him. Putting my trust in him, I was able to see Verlinda as a challenge to glorify him. She was a talent that belonged to Jesus. I would like to think that when we meet face to face, he will say, "Well done, good and faithful servant; enter into the joy of your master."

# 16

# Pass It Along

*Give happily to those in need,
always being ready to share with others
whatever God has given.*
1 TIMOTHY 6:18, TLB

At one time the speech department at the Watson Home was made up of three rooms. There was a small office, a large room used for gross-motor activities or groups, and a smaller room adaptable to two or three children receiving perception training and developing fine-motor skills, such as block patterns and peg board games. Except when working with children on chalkboard exercises or gross-motor activities such as crawling, creeping, jumping, and walking, I was usually in the small room.

One morning while I was there working with Patty, Anne Gray was working on the other side of the folding door with five teenagers who came each day for speech therapy. These children of normal intelligence had cerebral palsy. They were severely handicapped, and those who were able to speak at all were very difficult to understand.

While working with Patty that morning, I heard Anne begin the speech session by telling the five children the story of Samuel, how God called him three times and how Samuel finally answered: "Speak, for thy servant hears." She was working on the "S" sound with them.

Suddenly a thought came to me, and I called through the door to Anne, "Why don't we pray with those kids when they come for speech?"

Anne cut the therapy session short so we could discuss my suggestion. The five children were enthusiastic, and we agreed to talk about it the next day.

The following day we gathered in the small room feeling like conspirators as we worked out our plans. The small room had no windows, so we had the privacy we felt was necessary. We feared that praying with the children might be looked upon with disfavor by others.

We began meeting with them almost daily for prayer as part of each therapy session. I referred to it as a prayer group and told them about our prayer group at St. Stephen's Church, but the five young people would have none of that. They wanted it to be their "Prayer *Club*," so that it became. Thus began one of the most rewarding experiences of my life.

These young people in their early teens were just beginning to realize that their lives were going to be very different from the lives of normal teenagers. Like their peers without handicaps, they were beginning to be very self-conscious about their appearance, thinking about dating. But they also realized that their lives were not going to blossom as would the lives of their brothers and sisters and friends at home. Would they marry? Have babies? Probably not. What would become of them? It was a painful stage.

The teens in the Prayer Club responded freely to prayer. The first big sorrow we weathered was the death of Harry's grandmother. We all realized God's comforting love during that time and knew it was important for us to bring all our hurts to him.

We also prayed for a dream we shared—a dream of starting a home for severely handicapped and retarded children. This home would be run by Christian people and would provide employment opportunities for older and less disabled people such as our Prayer Club teens. We prayed for national and worldwide situations, for floods and other disasters. The children were not limited in their concerns to the local and familiar.

Birthdays became special occasions as we shared inspirational messages with the birthday person, either from the Bible or from our hearts. Harry's choice of Scripture on my birthday in 1962 was from Romans 8:17-18 and 2 Corinthians 4:17-18 (KJV).

> If children, then heirs; heirs of God, and joint-heirs with Christ; if so be that we suffer with him, that we may be also glorified together. For I reckon that the sufferings of this present time are not worthy to be compared with the glory which shall be revealed in us.
>
> For our light affliction, which is but for a moment, worketh for us a far more exceeding and eternal weight of glory . . . The things which are not seen are eternal.

The clear perspective he had on our true situation—not just the outward appearances—was profound! Another year Harry offered a message from his own heart.

## Why I Love God

God has a special meaning to me.
He is not only a spirit which the Bible says He is,
He is also a friend in need.

When I have a problem, I leave it in God's hands,
And He always helps me out of it.
And when I need someone to talk to,
I always have a friend.

The Prayer Club helped these young people, but it also ministered to me. There were times when I allowed the light of Christ that was in me to be hidden under layers of material concerns, busyness, or ugly resentments and other sins of the spirit. But somehow praying with these young people broke through to me. They helped me learn the truth about myself and to have the courage to do something about changing those things that hid the light of Christ in me. It was impossible to take my problems too seriously when I was with the Prayer Club. Their problems were so much greater than anything I had to deal with, and yet they left them in God's hands with a trusting faith.

One summer Anne and I hired the five Prayer Club members to help monitor a group of children who had severe emotional problems, some who were autistic. Their problems were very complex, and it was extremely difficult to gain the control needed to help them listen and learn.

However, we had noticed that these children seemed to relate to our five teenagers, and so we decided to see what would happen if the five had an opportunity to spend a period of four weeks with the younger children. Their effectiveness was particularly impressive during the children's afternoon rest period. Each of the five teens took responsibility for one child, to see that he or she remained on a cot for the required nap time. Without exception this proved to be successful. Although the children knew that the teens couldn't get out of their wheelchairs and run after them, there was something which held the children and kept them from trying to run off as they did when watched over by a nondisabled person. I believe the children knew that the teens loved them in a special way and sensed that their own problems and frustrations were less in comparison.

As for the teens, they discovered skills in themselves which they did not know they possessed, and they received their first paychecks for work well done. They realized, too, that through their work they were serving the Lord.

During my early years of involvement in the lives of the children at the Watson Home—of knowing their parents and feeling their hurt—Anne, Theo, and I began to think more and more about ways to help the whole family. We wondered about the difficulties they faced in such taken-for-granted areas as family vacations. Was it hard to find places where a family could go to enjoy a time away from home, a place at the seashore or a lake where they could swim or take walks and not be stared at because of their different child?

It seemed unfair that our sixty-six acres of land was so restricted in its zoning regulations. We couldn't develop anything on our property other than family dwellings. But there was a small house that had been occupied at one time by the man who watched over our Guernsey cows. Henry and I decided it would be an ideal vacation home.

We found a contractor who added a first floor bathroom equipped with special features for the handicapped. And Anne, Theo, and I painted the walls and furnished the place with "early attic" and other repaired items. It wasn't long before the "little house" was well equipped.

We couldn't wait for the first family to move in. Our dear friend Sam Odom came, and we had a service of blessing and prayers in the living room, asking God to be present in that home and with the families who would be using it.

For several years there were families who came each summer. It was a delight to see them enjoy our swimming pool, the paddle tennis court, picking vegetables on the farm, or just sitting on the porch enjoying the quiet of the country in peace and privacy.

One summer Pepé DaVia, a young man with cerebral palsy from Bogotá, Colombia, stayed at the little house with his mother, Daisy. He was a patient at the Watson Home and was assigned to the speech department. Though Pepé was blessed with a fine mind and a talent for painting, Anne Gray and I wondered how we would manage to give speech therapy in Spanish. Would we have to learn the language? As it turned out, Pepé understood and spoke several languages, one of which was English, so that problem was speedily overcome!

Pepé stayed for two years, and we became very devoted to him and Daisy. When they returned to Bogotá they invited Anne and me to come there to establish a speech and perception program at Propace. Propace, which they and other members of their family had been instrumental in founding, was a center for children with cerebral palsy who were from families too poor to pay for therapy.

Anne and I accepted the invitation with enthusiasm, arranged to go in July 1967, and spent several weeks prior to that learning how to speak Spanish—or so we thought!

Our month in Bogotá with Pepé and his family was a wonderful experience. We spent part of each day at the center, testing the children and setting up programs for them in speech and perception, language development, and in the areas of gross and fine motor skills. In the later afternoon we often visited museums and historical landmarks, shops, and other places of interest. We were impressed with the beauty of the country and the warmth and friendliness of the people we met.

That Bogotá trip and our association with Pepé and his family would never have happened without Verlinda. I wanted so much for her to know how much that meant to me.

Henry and I might have gone to Colombia as tourists and seen the museums and all the historical monuments; we could have eaten at the finest restaurants and possibly met some of the Colombian people, but nothing could have duplicated the experience of living with a family, meeting their friends, and being part of the creative work of helping the children of Propace and providing new ideas for the staff. Nothing can take away the deep sense of worth which that experience created in me.

Although the little house on our Dundee Farm is no longer used as a vacation house for families of handicapped children, it continues to be a blessing in the lives of others, helping to fill hospitality needs of various kinds.

While the fabric of our marriage was at one time in danger of being ripped apart because of the changes brought about by Verlinda, Henry and I look back now over the years and see how God has blessed our life together as he has taught us to be good stewards of all that he has given us. We are thankful for the many ways we are able to share our property and home with our Christian brothers and sisters. God can bring about the miracle of reconciliation if we give our lives and all we possess to him.

# 17
# Is Suffering God's Will?

*Thy kingdom come,*
*Thy will be done.*
MATTHEW 6:10

In the early days of grieving without hope over Verlinda's condition, I often wondered about the reason why. Was it the will of God? Some people said it was. At that point I couldn't disagree with them because I had no foundation, no basis for denying that view of God—I knew so little about him.

But after I came to faith in Christ and experienced the out-pouring of his love, I no longer believed that Verlinda had been struck down by a God who had willed that she live out her life on this earth with a severely impaired mind and body. She was his child, and if God was love, how could he will such an affliction on one of his children? Did he want the rest of us to learn a lesson? Was it a judgment or punishment on me for past sin? Was it, in fact, his will?

As I immersed myself more and more in his Word, read and reread the accounts of Jesus healing all those who came to him, I began to build a foundation upon which rested a firm conviction that God's will for all of us is wholeness.

God created the world with wholeness in mind. He created us in his own image, "In the image of God he created him; male and female he created them . . . And God saw everything that he had made, and behold, it was very good" (Genesis 1:27, 31).

We can't deny that God's original plan and will for us was wholeness without denying the authority of Scripture. So what happened? Why aren't we whole and well and without sickness and pain in our lives?

We know the story of Adam and Eve, how they were tempted and fell and were no longer whole and perfect the way God had created them to be. That story is our answer. As a result, we live in a fallen world plagued by Satan. We are subject to sickness and disease that has been in the world ever since man, by his own free will, fell from grace and forfeited God's plan and will for his wholeness.

So I deny that God's will for Verlinda was anything but wholeness. However, because she was part of the human family, she was subject to the results of the human family's free will throughout all generations. Since we as a people chose the way of death instead of life (and each human throughout history—other than Jesus—has continued to confirm that choice), the results can find their immediate expression in anyone.

Jesus Christ came to show us the Father, to tell us what the Father is like. What did he show us? Did he go about Galilee inflicting sickness, blindness, disease? Did he cause those who came to him walking to go away crippled? Did he fill emotionally sound people with demons and send them away screaming? Or did he heal the woman who had been plagued with an infirmity for eighteen years and say to those who criticized him, "Ought not this woman, a daughter of Abraham, *whom Satan bound for eighteen years,* be loosed from this bond?" (Luke 13:16, my italics).

Jesus said in John 4:34, "My food is to do the will of him who sent me," and again in John 5:30, "I seek not my own will but the will of him who sent me." In John 6:38 he says, "For I have come down from heaven, not to do my own will, but the will of him who sent me." If God had willed sickness and affliction, why was Jesus healing?

If Jesus had not healed people, we would have every right to say sadly to someone suffering a terminal illness or a crippling condition, "God's will be done." But thanks be to God, we read in the Gospels over and over again how Jesus healed "every disease and every infirmity" (Matthew 9:35) and "the blind receive their sight and the lame walk, lepers are cleansed and the deaf hear, and the dead are raised up" (Matthew 11:5). Jesus said this to prove that he was the Christ, the Messiah, God's Son who came to show us the Father.

In Acts 10:38 Peter told "how God anointed Jesus of Nazareth with the Holy Spirit and with power; how he went about doing good and healing all that were oppressed by the devil, for God was with him."

God's will for wholeness was still being carried out in the first century by Jesus' disciples, who were empowered by the Holy Spirit to do the works of the Father as Jesus had shown them.

In Luke 9:1-2 Christ commissioned his disciples to heal the sick: "And he called the twelve together and gave them power and authority over all demons and to cure diseases, and he sent them out to preach the kingdom of God and to heal." And again in Luke 10:1-9:

> After this the Lord appointed seventy others, and sent them on ahead of him . . . And he said to them . . . "Whenever you enter a town and they receive you, eat what is set before you; heal the sick in it and say to them, 'The Kingdom of God has come near to you.'"

Don't the Scriptures show that Jesus wanted his followers to carry on the work that he did? Jesus Christ came to redeem us and to show us what God was like. The greater part of his three year ministry was spent in healing every manner of sickness and disease. His life and ministry are proof to us that his Father's will is for wholeness of mind, body, and spirit.

To believe that God disciplines his children by afflicting us with the pains and grief of this present world is to compare him to a father who beats his child into submission by various forms of child abuse. Afflictions come, and God permits them. He uses them to draw us closer to himself, but he also causes all things to work together for good to those who love him (see Romans 8:28).

Some people are afraid to pray for healing or to encourage others to believe in God's power to heal. Indeed, a lack of faith in God's healing power and in his will for wholeness permeates every area of the human family. Many of the clergy throughout the history of the church have taught that "God's will be done" meant that *he* had laid our affliction upon us.

But how could a loving God who claims to be our Father do such a thing to one of his children? I do not believe that I could love God if he was like that, and further, if he had willed Verlinda to be the way she was, what was the point of doing anything to help her? If God wanted her to be that way, who was I to go against his will?

Of course, as we prayed for healing there was always the possibility that healing would not come, and those who were involved might thereby lose their faith. Perhaps that can happen, and it is a risk. But as I see it, the alternative is far worse. The desire of our hearts is to pray when sickness or disaster comes, even for those who have never turned to God before.

Through prayer, God can lead us to a place of knowing that the most important thing in our lives is our relationship to Jesus Christ. Then we can let go of our anxiety and put ourselves and those we love into his hands, knowing that whether we are healed or not is secondary in importance to receiving the gift of eternal life and living the life of quality which this relationship gives.

A letter from Dr. Hudson Taylor, the great missionary from England who founded the China Inland Mission in the latter half of the nineteenth century, is quoted in his biography, *Hudson Taylor's Spiritual Secret*. In spite of the deep grief he was experiencing over the death of his wife and infant son during an epidemic of cholera, he was able to write these words of faith to a friend:

> When I think of my loss, my heart, nigh to breaking, rises in thankfulness to him who has spared her such sorrow and made her so unspeakably happy. My tears are more tears of joy than grief. But most of all, I joy in God through our Lord Jesus Christ—in his works, his ways, his providence, himself. He is giving me to "prove" (to know by trial) "what is that good and acceptable, and perfect, will of God." I do rejoice in that will; it is acceptable to me; it is perfect; it is love in action. And soon, in that sweet will, we shall be reunited to part no more. (Dr. and Mrs. Howard Taylor, *Hudson Taylor's Spiritual Secret*, Chicago: Moody Press, 1932.)

This is the kind of faith that lives in the present and looks to the future knowing that God's plan for us is perfect.

I have often thought about the power that could be generated if all the parents of disabled and retarded children would pray in faith, believing in God's will for wholeness. I have imagined us praying together, expecting healing and wholeness for our children, believing it is God's will for them to be well. Christ told us that we could do even greater works than he did if we abide in him and let his words abide in us. But can these words abide in us if we are filled with the negative belief that God has willed our children to be afflicted?

Pray for wholeness, for God's will to be done. How can we know how far-reaching our prayers will be? Perhaps a doctor or therapist will receive such light from God that it will bring wholeness to many children through a new medicine or type of therapy. Or perhaps through our prayers of faith someone will receive the gift of God's healing power and become a channel through which it flows, increasing the knowledge and understanding of many as their eyes are opened to God's desire for wholeness. Pray for the many people who have been close to the retarded and don't see the disabled as a vital and important part of God's family. Our prayers can reach out to bring them to a greater understanding of and love for the "least" of his family.

Our persevering prayers really count! James tells us that "the prayer of a righteous man has great power in its effects" (James 5:16). But there is so much unbelief to overcome.

I have read many books on healing and of the wonderful miracles that have come about at gatherings of people of faith. And I have attended many services of healing and have been a witness to the deaf receiving their hearing or the lame walking. Even though I do not understand the mystery of why some are healed and some are not, I believe in the power of God working at these places. It seems to work because people have gone there in faith and expectancy. I have read that because most people there are praying with faith, the spiritual climate for healing is tremendous. That is a channel through which God can work.

But it is also important for us to embrace pain when it comes, to acknowledge it, and to lift it up in prayer. Once we have offered our pain to God, then we can look to see where we can be helpful, not only in weeping with them that weep (Romans 12:15), but in sharing the knowledge that "suffering produces endurance, and endurance produces character, and character produces hope, and hope does not disappoint us, because God's love has been poured into our hearts through the Holy Spirit which has been given to us" (Romans 5:3-5).

# 18
# Wholeness At Last

*So we know and believe the love God has for us.
God is love, and he who abides in love abides in God,
and God abides in him.*
1 JOHN 4:16

Many people hold the belief that God has given some of his children a severe physical or mental handicap or deformity of some kind because he loves them so much. Or again, some think that he has singled out particular families, sending them a handicapped child because he knows they have an extra capacity for love and will be able to pour out this special love upon their special child.

This concept of God working in our lives may bring an initial comfort, but it holds no lasting truth and its only appeal is to pride. One only has to go beyond this ideal to see families with a handicapped child who were destroyed by the tragedy, or the parents who are alcohol and drug abusers and have given birth to a child with brain damage as a result. Has God given *them* a "special" child because they have an extra capacity to love that child?

Hardly. There is nothing foolish or sentimental about God. He created the world according to his law, and it was good and orderly. It is the free will and disobedience of humans that destroyed that orderliness and goodness.

Leslie Weatherhead, in *The Will of God*, speaks of God's intentional will, his circumstantial will, and his ultimate will. Although I am not a theologian, my own experience of suffering brought me to similar insights about the way God works. I believe that he has shown me, as he promised he would, certain elements of truth.

Like Dr. Weatherhead, I believe that God did not *cause* the condition that resulted in Verlinda's severe brain damage. There were simply natural laws in the scheme of things, the incompatibility of two types of blood: one positive and one negative. Medical research had already discovered a solution to this incompatibility—the exchange blood transfusion immediately following the baby's birth. I can see God's will in that solution as he continues to work through men and women to bring about wholeness and answers to sickness and disease.

I cannot see God's will in the cause of the wrong report on my blood test prior to Verlinda's birth. The test was given to determine whether my blood was Rh-positive or Rh-negative. The report, either due to chance or to carelessness on someone's part, wrongly declared my blood type to be positive. I cannot see a loving God planning this because he wanted Henry and me to have a special baby upon whom we could lavish a special love and concern, or because we were a family with the means to provide special care for her and a special person, Margaret, to administer that care.

God's *intentional* will and ideal plan was for us to have a baby that was whole and well. This did not happen. Circumstances intervened, so God's *circumstantial* will came into being. Then, working his *ultimate* will, he acted through the circumstance of Verlinda's handicapped mind and body which brought me through hopelessness to the place where I saw that he was with us and that he was indeed a God of love. I began to understand that he felt my pain and that it was a sorrow to him, too, to have one of his children living in a spastic body.

"But," you might ask, "wouldn't it have been more loving if he would have just healed Verlinda outright?" I don't know the answer to that and don't expect to until I see him face to face.

I do know that I am thankful for the privilege of knowing and being part of the world of the disabled. I know that God brought good out of the evil of sickness not only to me but to many others and it has been enough to know that he is in charge. His thoughts are not my thoughts, nor his ways my ways, for he said, "as the heavens are higher than the earth, so are my ways higher than your ways and my thoughts than your thoughts" (Isaiah 55:9). It has been enough to know that God did not will Verlinda's condition or the condition of all those similarly afflicted, because he *is* love. Love is perfect, and therefore love is *not* sickness. That knowledge gave me the freedom to pray, believing that I was aligning myself with the will of God instead of going against it.

Father John Banks wrote in his book, *Healing Everywhere*: "No one of us is entirely unrelated to this task of healing. This is a very sick world. Are you part of the disease? Or are you part of the cure? *The goal of divine healing is the demonstrating in human experience of the kingdom of God*" (San Diego: St. Luke's Press, 1953).

As God works in the circumstances of our lives, he reveals to us that nothing needs to be wasted. When we entrust our lives to him, we see that he has always been at work in those circumstances. As we see his plan for our lives unfold, we understand that he is always working toward his ultimate will for us, which is our redemption by his love through Jesus Christ.

This is the central focus of the gospel of Jesus Christ. It is not his ministry of healing, although that is an important part, a part that expresses God's love and is a part we need to believe. But the *full* gospel is in receiving the free gift of eternal life, in repentance, and in acknowledging that Jesus Christ died that we might live, forgiven and made righteous in the sight of God.

For our life and for Verlinda's I believe that . . .

- God's *intentional* will was that we would have a healthy, happy baby.
- God's *circumstantial* will, however, had already established certain cause and effect natural laws that collided to produce her handicap and our sorrow.
- God's *ultimate* will was her and our complete redemption.

We might have hoped for that redemption to include healing and wholeness in this life. But we must remember that ultimate redemption is union with God, and, as Paul said, "this slight momentary affliction is preparing for us an eternal weight of glory beyond all comparison" (2 Corinthians 4:17).

God's ultimate will for Verlinda was fulfilled in her twenty-seventh year. She is now with him in his kingdom. When she died she received the new and perfect body God intended her to have from the beginning. Throughout her life there were many times when we wondered if she would survive the high fevers, convulsions, and other complications. She never weighed more than forty-four pounds. With so little physical resistance, she was often close to death.

Her passing from this life in her limited body and mind through death and into life in her new body was very peaceful. Her death came unexpectedly. There was no struggle, no illness. She just stopped breathing one Sunday afternoon. Her work here was finished.

Verlinda was staying at the Watson Home at the time of her death. Margaret was away on her vacation, and we were taking the opportunity to have Verlinda's bedroom and bathroom repapered and painted. I had visited her on Friday and expected to see her again Sunday. However, I received a call from Harry, my "prayer club" friend, asking me to meet him for a visit at the airport Sunday afternoon. I agreed, thinking I'd see Verlinda again soon enough.

But the telephone rang about 5:30 that evening. It was Mrs. Wright, the director of nursing at the Home. "Mrs. Chalfant," she said, "can you come over? Dolly isn't feeling well, and I think you should get here as soon as you can."

"We'll be right there," I said.

Henry and I drove to the Home sensing that it was serious, even suspecting her death. Mrs. Wright met us in the lobby and told us that Verlinda was dead. She explained: "Dolly had been resting on the bed in her braces, and the nurse had just gotten her up for her supper. She was sitting in her chair. The nurse turned away to get her tray, and when she turned back, she saw that Dolly had stopped breathing. It all happened so quietly and quickly. We called the doctor right away, and he's there now. He said there wasn't anything we could have done."

As we entered the unit where Verlinda had been staying, we saw her lying on her bed as though asleep. She seemed very peaceful. One of the nurses remarked that she thought Verlinda must have been homesick and lonely. I thought about how I could have come to see her instead of visiting Harry at the airport. A load of guilt descended upon me. "Poor Dolly," I thought, "she must have felt deserted by us all. No Margie, no Mum Mum."

For two days I carried that guilt, and then it lifted. I remembered that God was love. Nothing could separate us from that love or the truth that we loved Dolly and wanted the best for her. Nothing could change the truth that she had been in God's care since the day she was conceived and that her life had been a blessing and pro-

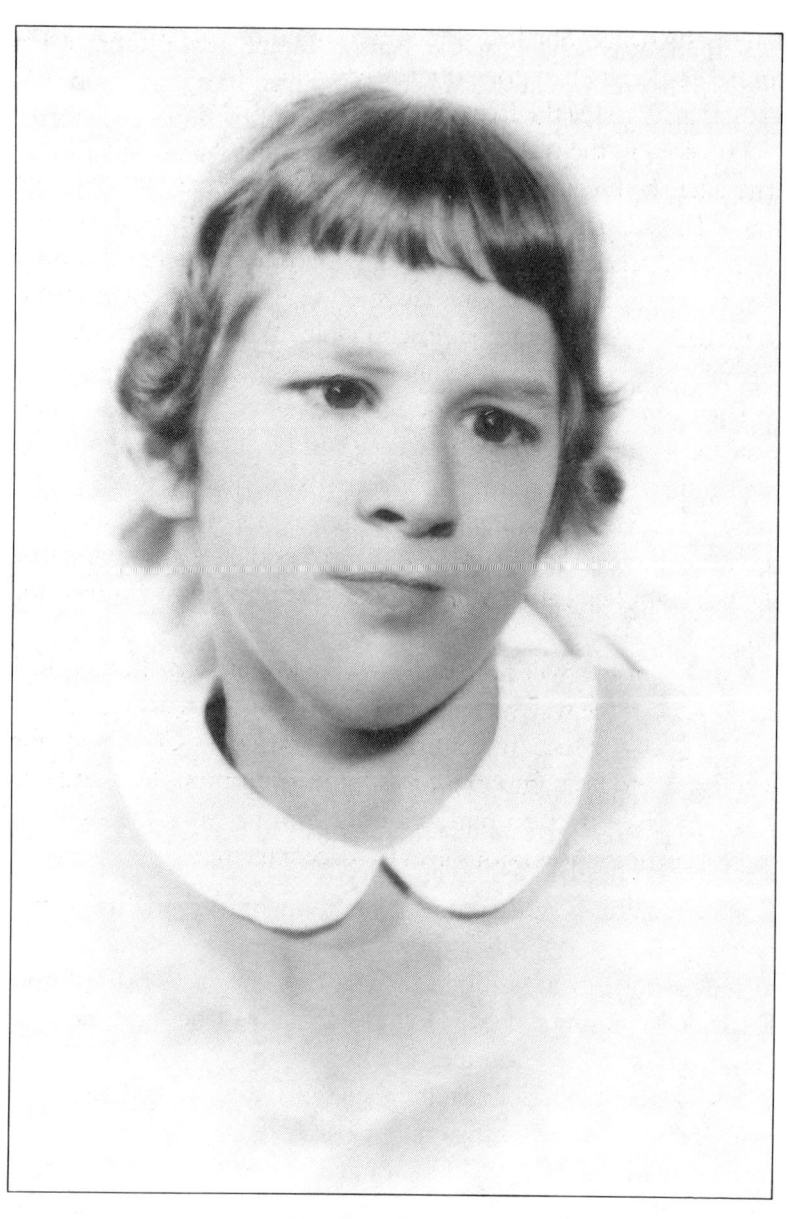

*Portrait of Verlinda*

found experience. She had simply accomplished the work God had for her to do and had gone home to be with him. She was the first in our family to see the face of Jesus.

I rejoiced in the reality of her new body, but it wasn't until two days after the funeral service that I realized what that meant. There was a Thursday morning service of Holy Communion at St. Stephen's, the service that grew out of Bishop Pardue's prayer group twenty-four years earlier. Our daughter Anne, Margaret, and I went to the service, needing to be close to Dolly. While I was kneeling at the rail, I tried to visualize Verlinda, but her image eluded me.

Then I *saw* her as she is now in her new body, a lovely young woman, the daughter I would know and be able to communicate with someday in heaven. The vision passed quickly through my mind, but it was an assurance to me that all was well with her, that the years she spent in the prison of her old body were over, and that she was with her Father who loved her and his Son who died for her.

God's ultimate will for her had prevailed, and her healing had come—not in the way we had prayed for those many years, but real healing, nonetheless. It confirmed my belief in God's will for wholeness and how important it is for us to turn our lives and our children's lives over to him, allowing him to work through the painful circumstances of our lives to redeem them.

# 19
# A Life Fulfilled

*I am the resurrection and the life,
he who believes in me, though he die,
yet shall he live.*
JOHN 11:25

Verlinda's funeral took place at St. Stephen's Church on August 22, 1973. Anne, Henry, Jr. and his family, and Nancy all returned home as soon as they heard of their sister's death. Margaret, whose life was the most drastically changed by Verlinda's death, was also able to come back from her vacation.

Friends and family expressed their sympathy in thoughtful ways. We received many notes, some from people who had found it difficult to acknowledge Verlinda's existence when she was alive but who were able to express their love to us after her death. There were many from people who knew Verlinda, some who had retarded children themselves, others who knew her through their work with the handicapped. The theme in most of the notes was about the good that had come out of the life of one so handicapped.

The service for Verlinda suggested the same theme, that "all things work together for good to them that love God" (Romans 8:28).

On the morning following Verlinda's death I was reading Psalm 20. This passage had been unfamiliar to me, but as soon as I read it, I knew that it applied to Dolly. So we incorporated the first five verses into her funeral.

> In your day of trouble, may the Lord be with you! May the God of Jacob keep you from all harm. May he send you aid from his sanctuary in Zion. May he remember with pleasure the gifts you have given him, your sacrifices and burnt offerings. May he grant you your heart's desire and fulfill all your plans. May there be shouts of joy when we hear the news of your victory, flags flying with praise to God for all that he has done for you. May he answer all your prayers. (TLB)

What could be more appropriate than God remembering with pleasure Dolly's sacrifices and burnt offerings of pain and disability, or that there would be shouts of joy over her victory?

But in the days that followed, my thoughts rambled and groped. I grieved for Verlinda—not in the same way I had grieved when we were told she was hopelessly retarded; that was a shattering grief without hope. At her death it was a time of quiet sadness mixed with joy, knowing that we would miss her but being thankful that she didn't have to live in pain and discomfort any longer. In the last few years of her life she had been less relaxed, more often rigid and spastic, and the mild seizures had started up again. I believe she was ready to go when she died.

I also experienced a feeling of relief, knowing that her struggle and ours were at an end. It seemed good to look ahead to a less complicated life, to times when we wouldn't have to plan out every detail of every day.

Later I realized that if something seems to be too much of a burden to bear and the tension continues over a period of time, it can help to think what it would be like to be completely without that burden for the rest of your life. Paul tells us to be content in whatever situation we find ourselves, and now I understand the wisdom of that advice. Each situation has its challenges and its blessings. With Dolly the challenges were great, but when she was gone, I wondered what I had that was unique and particularly mine? Nothing. It was all gone—the difference, the struggle, the tension, the caring and planning.

Once there were times when I longed for the freedom of not having a handicapped child, to be able to live like other people. Finally I was free. "Freedom's just another word for nothing left to lose," sang Janis Joplin. And I discovered she knew what she was talking about. What purpose was there in my life after having been motivated for so long by the purpose of Dolly's life? How could I suddenly switch to a new motivation? I felt deprived, less than whole, and guilty for ever having thought it was too much to have her at home all the time.

I'd like to pretend now that I never had those feelings, but they were something I had to face. It was all very well to say that Dolly was better off and at peace and all those things we knew were true at the funeral, but those words didn't relieve the ache that began to develop in the days that followed.

Verlinda's life was like a ball—completely round with no chronological milestones. And then suddenly, it was finished. Could we ever have known her thoughts, or did she even have any? She did have some response to communication and to prayer. But did she know who we were? I think so. I hope so.

Now I can feel her maturity. She knows us. She's no longer a child, no longer utterly dependent, but a young woman. I'm her mother, and I can sense it. Whatever good came out of Dolly's life was God working—proof that the weaker we are, the more he can work through us. Dolly was totally disabled. Who could be weaker than that?

Thomas Traherne, in his *Centuries of Meditations* says,

> Prize it now you have it, at that rate and you shall be a grateful creature: nay, you shall be a divine and heavenly person. For they in heaven do prize blessings when they have them. They in earth, when they have them, prize them not; they in hell prize them when they have them not.
>
> To have blessings and to prize them is to be in heaven; to have them and not to prize them is to be in hell, I would say upon earth: To prize them and not to have them, is to be in hell (London: Bertram Dobell, 1908).

My heavenly times with Verlinda were when I was close to God and realized Verlinda was a child of God. When I did not see her as a blessing and was not at peace with myself or with God, I made my own hell. To wish she were back was a way to create another kind of hell, filled with guilt and far removed from the kingdom of heaven. The kingdom of heaven is at hand when we see ourselves in God's hands whether we are in this world or the next.

"When the perishable puts on the imperishable, and the mortal puts on immortality, then shall come to pass the saying that is written: 'Death is swallowed up in victory!'" (1 Corinthians 15:54).

# 20
# Verland

*So shall my word be that goes forth from my mouth;
it shall not return to me empty, but it shall accomplish
that which I purpose, and prosper
in the thing for which I sent it.*
ISAIAH 55:11

God works in mysterious ways, bringing together various people and ideas to accomplish his will. We saw him work in a special way in the founding of the Verland Foundation, a residence for the profoundly retarded.

When Andrew Hanzel was admitted to Western Center, his mother, Theo applied for work there, too. She was employed as a nurse's aide and started working with forty very difficult boys.

Carol Mitchell was also employed at Western Center as an aide. One of the difficult boys with whom both Theo and Carol worked was David Tresch; he was a handsome blond youngster who was a self-abuser and beat himself unmercifully about the face and head. Carol and Theo were both committed to helping David overcome this destructive behavior and eventually succeeded. It was through David that Carol and Theo became close friends. And it was through Theo that I got to know Carol.

Carol later earned a bachelor's degree in psychology and went on for her masters in administration. She eventually became the administrator of the Allegheny Valley Junior School, a private facility for the profoundly retarded. It was housed in an old building that was soon to be condemned, and the board decided not to build a new facility but to concentrate their efforts on the senior division of the school.

Devastated by the prospect of closing this home for a hundred profoundly retarded people, Carol came to our house the night the board made its final decision. We talked far into the night and finally decided that, through faith and trust in God, we would form a new corporation, one that would build a new environment in which the residents would have as home-like an atmosphere as possible.

We marveled at God's hand in all of this—Andrew and Verlinda brought Theo and me together, David brought Carol into Theo's life and subsequently into mine. We tried a variety of ways to incorporate the names Verlinda, Andrew, and David and finally decided on Verland.

Carol went home relieved, knowing that no matter what difficulties lay ahead, David and the other residents would not be abandoned.

Soon Carol learned of some property on a hilltop near Sewickley owned by Helen Grove. For many years Helen had been deeply concerned for the needs of young people and had been affiliated with Youth Guidance, Inc., in its efforts to match troubled children one-on-one with volunteers who could befriend them and introduce them to Jesus Christ.

When Carol explained our needs for a new facility, Helen was immediately interested and said, "I have been praying about what to do with my property. I believe this land belongs to God, and it would be a great joy to me to know that he wants me to use it in such a way. I would like to give it to you in honor of my husband, Don." God's mysterious ways are wonderful ways!

So it came about that thirteen acres of wooded land overlooking a pond were donated to Verland by this lovely Christian woman. We knew that only the power of prayer and faith in God could have brought about such a miracle.

In May, 1978, the Verland Foundation, Inc., was officially organized, and soon thereafter a temporary occupancy extension was granted to Verland to operate a seventy-bed interim-care facility in the old Allegheny Valley Junior School for the lowest functioning and most physically handicapped of the former one hundred residents. The remaining thirty were placed in private facilities, group homes, and State Centers.

A busy time for Carol and the new board began. Many decisions had to be made. We moved ahead with architectural plans for the new facility and the sale of tax-exempt revenue bonds to provide the funds for such an undertaking. On the day before Thanksgiving in 1979 we had a ground-breaking ceremony in the woods overlooking the pond on Helen Grove's property. Some rough times had preceded this day when it appeared that some people in the community would not accept such a facility in their midst. It was difficult to convince them that the people we served were not mentally deranged, that they would not be roaming through the neighborhood frightening children or being destructive in other ways.

Many of the residents were confined to wheelchairs, others were blind, and all needed total supervision. They were not capable of running about on their own. Several town meetings were held and many prayers said before approval was given. But once again God was faithful, and one more step brought us closer to our goal.

Verland's mission was to provide a life with dignity to the least capable retarded or developmentally disabled person in the most normal community setting possible. Therefore ten homes were built, each constructed to house nine residents eventually. The plans also included three other buildings, each one honoring one of the three special children who had brought Carol, Theo, and me together. They were the David W. Tresch Administration Building, the Andrew Hanzel Central Services Building, and the Verlinda M. Chalfant Activities Center.

Verland opened its doors to the residents in January, 1981. A cold and difficult winter followed as the staff struggled to adjust to living under separate roofs. There is no question that an institutional setting housed in one building is easier to operate than decentralized homes. Nurses and supervisors can go from ward to ward to make rounds without having to brave all kinds of weather. The residents do not have to be dressed in outer clothing, mittens, and hats on a cold morning just to go to their activities in another building, and they do not have to be pushed in heavy wheelchairs through snow or rain to get to the gym, etc. Frustration levels rose and sometimes exploded.

But gradually, it became apparent that the residents were responding to the homey environment. Their health improved as they were moved about in the fresh air. Those who could walk improved physically, and some who previously had not walked began to take steps. They responded to the increased stimulation of their environment and in some cases became less lethargic.

I suppose a whole book could be written about Verland today and its residents. There is a charm to the houses, the sturdy furniture, and the lovely grounds. The activities center has classrooms, therapy rooms, a gymnasium, and a swimming pool with a ramp for the wheelchairs. When Verland opened its doors, each of the ten houses was managed by a live-in married couple—some with families of their own—who served as houseparents to the residents. However, the staffing patterns have changed. Now it is more difficult to find people to live there, so care of the residents is provided by three eight-hour shifts.

The daily routine of the residents is normal. Those attending school are dressed and readied by the house parents and other staff persons to go off to school in a special van or the school bus. The ones who are over the age of twenty-one go to the activities center for a program especially designed for their needs. They remain there until about three p.m., receiving their lunch there also. Those who are able benefit from the cafeteria where they choose their own menu from the selection provided. They are responsible for helping to clean up and put things away after their meal. Some of these older residents are learning to fold laundry and are encouraged to develop skills in other household activities.

Early in the summer of 1982, our committee for ministry with the disabled at St. Stephen's Church initiated a service at the church for the residents of Verland and other facilities for the retarded. Recently we changed the name from "The Verland Service" to "Joyful Noise Service"; and so it is—joyful as well as noisy!

At ten o'clock on Thursday mornings the congregation arrives. Those who can walk arrive in the orange school bus, and those in wheelchairs are brought in a van with a hydraulic lift. Staffing is almost one-to-one. The worship service lasts for about forty minutes.

The first time we gathered for this service, it was chaotic, or so it seemed to me. There were many sounds, screams, and inappropriate laughter. Some of the residents were unmanageable and had to be taken out. Everyone was tense, wondering how it would go. But I was touched so deeply that I started weeping and couldn't stop. I knew that had Verlinda been alive, she would have been included; she would have been a part of this time of recognition of the right of every human being to be seen in a place of worship as a child of God—worthy of the dignity and respect given to the "normal" population.

Since then all of us who are involved have become more comfortable with the worship service. We have lost the initial fear that it would be too difficult to sing above the other uncontrollable sounds or that the staff might resent the effort of bringing the residents out in all kinds of weather. We gradually lost our anxiety when a resident took a Bible or prayer book from the pew rack, afraid that he might rip it apart.

I was thinking of that just recently when I watched Michael, a tall handsome young man sitting by himself in the pew. He took a hymnal from the rack, flipped through the pages a few times and put it back. At the first service he had been so unruly that he had to be taken out. Now he walks in alone and has the inner control to sit by himself without someone monitoring his behavior.

Kathy has learned to sing "Jesus Loves Me," and sometimes Jimmy leads us in the Lord's Prayer.

These people teach us to lay down our lives in ways we never dreamed we could, and we learn something of real servanthood as we give without expecting anything in return.

Our rector John Guest said of the handicapped in a sermon he preached on Retardation Sunday, an annual event at St. Stephen's:

> Rather than our dignity being destroyed by involvement with them, our dignity is enlarged. The principle is this: what you give is what you get. If you despise people, you will be despised. Treat life cheaply, and life will be cheap to you. If you extend the indignity of wiping out life because it's not the kind of life that should be allowed to live, you cheapen your own life. *Your* life loses dignity.
>
> What you do, is what you become. If, when you suffer hardship, you embrace it, if you welcome adversity, you will become a person of character. Hide yourself as best you can from it—which is nearly impossible—and you will be consumed by it.
>
> None of us can escape pain, but how do we respond to it? If the Spirit of God indwells us, if we have been made new in Jesus

Christ, then Scripture exhorts us to face that hardship so that we can become men and women of character and share with others the comfort with which we have been comforted during it.

"Every one to whom much is given, of him will much be required" (Luke 12:48).

# 21
# Answered Prayers

*Or what man of you,
if his son asks him for bread,
will give him a stone?*
MATTHEW 7:9

There were times when I wondered why Verlinda was never healed during her life on earth. There were so many prayers offered on her behalf from the beginning of my new life in Christ—the prayer group at St. Stephen's, people like Father John Banks, who prayed and laid hands on her that she might be healed. The list is long, including leaders in the healing movement such as Agnes Sanford, Glenn Clark, Emily Gardiner Neal, Dr. Alfred Price, and others. We missed no opportunity to take Verlinda to them or invite them to our home for that purpose. Several times we took Verlinda to the services in Pittsburgh conducted by Kathryn Kuhlman, a dynamic woman who was used greatly by God to bring about many miracles of healing both in physical and spiritual ailments declared to be "hopeless."

When Verlinda was in her teens I remember talking to Sam Odom about why God wouldn't heal her.

"Would you really want him to now?" Sam asked me.

"Well, of course," I said, "Why wouldn't I?"

"Think about what it would be like for her," he answered. "It would be like moving into a totally strange environment. She would have no background of going to school or making friends. She has been a baby all these years while other children have been growing up. It would be very hard on her I should think."

This was something I had never thought of, but I could see there was some truth in what he had said. It *would* have been hard for her.

Still, there were many promises Jesus made that I wondered about. In John 15:7 Jesus said: "If you abide in me, and my words abide in you, ask whatever you will, and it shall be done for you." Wasn't I abiding in him and his words in me? What more should I be doing?

Jesus also said:

Ask, and it will be given you; seek, and you will find; knock, and it will be opened to you. For everyone who asks receives, and he who seeks finds, and to him who knocks it will be opened. Or what man of you, if his son asks him for bread, will give him a stone? Or if he asks for a fish, will give him a serpent? If you then, who are evil, know how to give good gifts to your children, how much more will your Father who is in heaven give good things to those who ask him! (Matthew 7:7-11).

I wondered about that; Verlinda's healing seemed to me to be a good gift, far better than having to live all those years in her spastic body. But as I look back on it, I know that God's plan for her and his gift to her were far better than anything I could have given to her. In comparison to eternity, twenty-six years was a very short span—a short time to wait for a new body and an everlasting life with him.

Now I know that her life was right the way it was. I learned so much, and I have been able to share with others what life with Dolly was like day in and day out. Moreover, I would never have learned patience, endurance, or the kind of courage I saw in people who faced severe handicaps day after day.

In seeking and knocking, many things of God were opened to me and continue to be opened, and I am thankful. Through the years I learned about prayer. Some say that it is selfish to pray for material or physical needs. But I believe they are putting limits on God's power. God wants us to turn to him no matter what our needs, and then he fills us with his grace and leads us into prayer that is more unselfish and selfless.

I had this experience in praying for Verlinda. My prayers for her at the beginning were for the most part selfish, being unselfish only in that I was praying for the healing of another human being. God recognized my prayers for what they were. I did not need to tell him all the selfish reasons involved. He knew them. But that did not prevent him from taking my prayers and guiding me into the more unselfish prayer of lifting all handicapped children to him in compassion and love.

Then he went a step further and brought children into my life who had similar handicaps for whom I could pray. These prayers were no longer selfish because, if I had wanted only my own ease, I could have walked away from those situations. But I discovered that others' needs were greater than my own. With God's help I was able to assist these children and their families through the weekend program at the Watson Home, fixing the little house on Dundee Farm for summer vacations, and other specific ways.

I saw my selfish prayers transformed. God hears our prayers, from the big altruistic ones to the small and selfish ones. Don't limit his power for fear that it is only right to pray for this or that. Just get on your knees and *pray* and let God do the rest. "Come to me, all who labor and are heavy laden, and I will give you rest" (Matthew 11:28). He invites us to come to him with our burdens, big and small, promising to refresh us. I know that he has been faithful to his promises. He is unchanging. Although it sometimes seems that he has not heard our prayers, I know that in the fullness of time they will be honored.

Others say we should no longer pray for God's healing power—as though it were something appropriate only in the years when Jesus walked on the earth. But this denies God's unchangeable character.

I may never have come to know God if I hadn't believed he was *able* to heal my child in this century. How could I have loved a God who had healed Peter's mother-in-law of a fever, the woman who suffered for twelve years from an infirmity, the child whose fits threw him into the fire, and the little girl he raised from the dead, but would not heal someone close to me because I happened to be born and live in another century, some 1,900 years too late? Is God fickle? Is he bound by time? Certainly not. "Jesus Christ is the same yesterday and today and for ever" (Hebrews 13:8). God does not change; we are told that his character includes steadfastness; he is "the Father of lights with whom there is no variation or shadow due to change" (James 1:17).

Why some are healed and some not will remain a mystery until we see him face to face. All of us who pray in faith for healing will always ask "why?" when healing does not come. It's okay to ask "why" if in the meantime we stay close to God, open to be channels for his compassion.

I experienced his compassion when I realized that I no longer saw Verlinda as a burden but as a blessing. When people referred to her as a burden, I had to remember that I thought of her that way once, too. There was never a break from the "burden" of planning and caring for the physical well-being of a retarded person, but through *prayer* and faith the burden of *grief* and the emotional burden no longer weighed me down. I received the blessing of joy in my heart, and the "peace of God, which passes all understanding" that Paul spoke of in Philippians 4:7.

I understood that God worked through Verlinda to reach others with his message of love for all humanity. I saw those close to her grow close to God, and I realized that God has a plan for all of us who offer our lives to him, even the least of us. God will not push us around; we choose to be in communication with him in prayer. A great responsibility lies with the parents of children who cannot reach out for themselves. We have to lift them in prayer and surround them with faith and love so that they can be receptive to God's plan for them.

At the time of Verlinda's birth, St. Stephen's Church had no pastor. Our call to Bishop Pardue when she became critically ill resulted in his ongoing interest in her. He prayed faithfully for her. Through the years of the bishop's ministry—through his preaching in all parts of the world, his weekly radio broadcast, and his books—he often spoke about Verlinda in relation to the importance of prayer.

Bishop Pardue was aware that Verlinda's problem differed more in degree than in kind from most of us who appear to have no handicap. He realized that we are all blind somewhere in our thinking and often deaf to God's Word. It wasn't Verlinda's eyes that made her blind but the inability to use them! Our spiritual eyes may be blinded in the same way.

"Verlinda," he wrote, "has influenced the lives of hundreds of people. Prayer groups and study groups have been formed through her fight toward victory. God alone knows how far her life has reached to give people a deeper understanding of the mystery of suffering."

My feeble and selfish prayers for Verlinda were the beginning.

God took them and multiplied them! I don't understand why he chose to answer them the way he did. I would have chosen healing and a normal life for Verlinda. But as I look back on my life, I would not change any part of it. God's hand never ceased to be in it. Verlinda's sacrifice was great, but the glory and honor she brought to Jesus Christ was greater.

I wrote the following in my journal on her birthday a few years after her death:

> This is Dolly's birthday. She would be thirty-four today. I wonder what our life would have been like with four normal children? Maybe we, like other families, would have numerous grandchildren now. What would *we* be like? All that grief and struggle, all that beauty would have been unknown to us. What a dear blessing her life was to so many. What a disruptive force it was; it blasted open everything that had gone before.
>
> Thanks to her I can read everything in the Bible with new eyes. Lord, thank you for the tremendous blessing she has been—despite all the heartache, the loss of normalcy for the family. Your grace came upon this house because of her. She is with you now, and some day we'll all be together in your heaven praising you in the company of angels and archangels. Thanks be to God!

# Epilogue

Five years have passed since I made my commitment to write this book, since I began to set aside each Wednesday to review my life and Verlinda's with the purpose of sharing with other parents the blessing and pain of having a profoundly retarded and multiply disabled child.

    I found the review rewarding; it brought me in touch with all of my life, the good and the bad. It inspired me to see God's hand in my life from the beginning. It was as though he had woven a tapestry from threads of different experiences, some dark and shadowy, some bright and glowing.

Even the years before I knew and loved the Lord were not wasted years. God took the inadequacies I felt as a girl and young woman and transformed them from self-pity to a sensitivity toward the handicapped and retarded, making it possible for me to relate lovingly to them and them to me. I knew something of how they felt.

Watchman Nee in his book of daily readings, *Through the Year with Watchman Nee*, speaks to that very point:

> All that happened to you before you were saved, as well as after, has some definite meaning. Whatever your character and temperament, whatever your strengths and weaknesses, all are pre-known by God and prepared by Him with future service in view. There is no accident, for everything is within God's providence. Nothing comes by chance.
>
> God does not write off as valueless our unregenerate days. He has a use for the persons we are and intends to use the real us, purified by the cross, and not some pretense, in His service (Eastbourne, East Sussex: Kingsway Publications, Ltd., 1977).

God's miracle of grace in my life demonstrates the truth of Isaiah 55:8 and 9: "For my thoughts are not your thoughts, neither are your ways my ways, says the Lord. For as the heavens are higher than the earth, so are my ways higher than your ways and my thoughts than your thoughts."

My comfort has been knowing that Verlinda's weakness became strength and that her life had a purpose in the kingdom of God.

I have written about my experiences. I do not claim to have the ultimate theology of suffering, nor do I say that my experience was the most profound. It was *mine*—unique to me, yet part of all the suffering and pain in this world. To one degree or another, we all feel helpless in the face of serious pain. We never want those we love to experience it. Our hearts are heavy when we hear about a per-

*Epilogue*

son's terminal illness, a plane crash in which many lives have been cut short, families lost in car wrecks, or the present tragedies of missing children and children on drugs. "How will their families deal with it?" we wonder. We think about people dying of hunger or the suffering of nations at war. The suffering in our world is more than we can comprehend.

I'm thankful to have experienced a small part of the world's pain. Now I know what it is to feel it, and it gives me a oneness with the suffering of so many others.

But most of all, I thank God that he gave me the greatest gift—the gift of his Son, Jesus Christ. The day my eyes were opened to him was the day I *could* share in the world's suffering, not as someone without hope, but as someone who knew that God was in control and who could comfort through the comfort I received from him.

Thanks be to God for his "unsearchable riches," for calling me "out of darkness into his marvelous light," that Christ might dwell in my heart through faith, to know the love of Christ which surpasses knowledge and to be filled with all the fullness of God.

> Lord, I thank you for the pain of Verlinda, for the victory of Verlinda in you, for the Door through which I walked to discover a new dimension of life. Thank you for the people on the other side of the Door, whom I would never have known without Verlinda. Above all I thank you for sending your Son, Jesus Christ, to die on the cross for me that I might become a new creation and enter into your kingdom.
>
> I love you and praise you and pray that what I have written on these pages will be pleasing to you and will bring honor and glory to you. I pray in the name of your beloved Son, my Lord and Savior, Jesus Christ. Amen.

# Appendix
# How the Church Can Help

Both Sam Odom and John Banks are examples of ministers who related positively to the needs of the retarded and their families. There are others, too, like John Guest, who understand the diversity of problems and the depth of grief that parents experience when they discover the hopelessness of a child's condition.

But in many cases, ministers and priests are quite unaware and untrained in the area of mental retardation and the effect it can have on a family. I was once told by a young Episcopal minister that he had received no teaching in seminary on the subject of retardation, and he admitted to having no skills to counsel parents of retarded children.

This is an area where your prayers can be effective. Parents can pray for changes to come about in seminaries so that ministry to families of the retarded and the retarded themselves will be included in the curriculum.

I had the opportunity a few years ago to speak to a group of seminary students about the importance of knowing how to minister to these families. I said, "Most ministers consider death to be the ultimate grief, especially the death of a child, but they don't know or understand the depth of grief and fear that the parents of a retarded child experience because it is unfamiliar ground to them."

## Understanding the Paradox of Grief and Bravery

The grief parents feel when their child's condition is revealed is as deep as though the child were dead. But most parents feel they have to hold their emotions in check, and pretend to be brave and hopeful. It's no wonder that parents are often unable to accept the fact of retardation at first. There are those who never arrive at real acceptance and never experience the comfort of loving their child just as he or she is.

## Important Assurances to Parents

A minister needs to know these things because families desperately need spiritual help and counsel at the beginning and throughout the years they are caring for their child.

A minister can assure the parents of a profoundly retarded or physically handicapped child of several things:

- God loves them and their child.
- God is not punishing them through their child.
- God did not send this child as a cross for them to bear.
- The condition of their child is a sorrow to God.
- He (the minister) loves them and understands their situation to the best of his ability.
- They and their child are welcome in church.

## Special Concerns That Need Pastoring

There are pitfalls waiting in the wings for the family with a retarded child. If the clergy are aware of these potential problem areas, they can do a great deal to help the family avoid them. The ongoing stress the parents face can be alleviated by friends in the church who want to help.

1. *Emotional distress and guilt* will often assail the family if the time comes when they have to make the dreaded decision of placing their child in an institution. The trauma experienced by these families requires the understanding of a pastor.

2. *Family breakup* is a very real possibility. Currently, the statistics on the break-up of families with a retarded child runs four out of five. It is generally the father who cannot take the stress and walks away from the problem. The mother, who usually has few resources, then falls back on her parents, leaving them to cope with a difficult situation while she tries to support her family.

3. *Unequal acceptance of the condition* can divide a couple when one parent accepts the condition of the child and the other refuses to or when the burden of care falls on the mother so heavily that it makes it impossible for her to have time left for the father or other children. If the marriage is already in a tenuous state, a disabled child will put it over the edge. Spiritual support and professional counsel can strengthen the relationship between husband and wife when it begins to crumble under the weight of problems produced by the pain and burden of a retarded child.

4. *Blame from relatives* increases stress. Sometimes the situation is worsened by grandparents who place blame on their son-in-law or daughter-in-law for the retardation. Or perhaps they refuse to accept the fact that their grandchild is retarded.

## Educating the Congregation

The way a family with a handicapped member is received in their church can dramatically affect whether the family will survive the trauma. Ministers can educate their parishioners regarding retardation and other disabilities. Here are some suggestions for pastors and lay leaders.

- Though adults know that retardation and disabilities are not contagious, children may need to be informed and educated.
- Teaching about kindness and thoughtfulness should not be neglected.
- Raise the church's consciousness about the value of every human life so people will resist the ideology of our day which suggests that some lives are not worth preserving.
- Quell any "bad theology" about handicaps and their causes.
- Encourage church members to be helpful to the family with a retarded child, to stay with the child sometimes so that the parents can have some relief from the tedium of daily schedules.
- Be informed about community programs for the retarded so you can make suggestions as to where the family can go to receive professional help.
- Take the lead in making sure the church building can accommodate the handicapped instead of resisting such alterations.

Educate the church to see these children as lovable and to recognize them as part of God's family, spiritual beings with as great a need for Christ in their lives as the rest of us. Provide education and programs for them. A church which welcomes all members of a family in spite of a severe disabling condition is a church where Jesus Christ would feel welcome.

**Influence in the Community**
Christians must be leaders in their communities in changing the public's attitudes about the disabled. Out of ignorance there are many who resist such things as opening group homes in their community or who stare and make rude comments when they see the

retarded "invading" the public space. It is the responsibility of our churches to educate and stimulate the community to understand and lovingly accept handicapped people. We must initiate and support programs that provide help for those who are retarded or disabled in any way.

There will always be some who resist and some who support, some who are fearful and some who understand. But the response of Christians to the problem of retardation and all disabilities is important. Other people look to us to see if our actions match our words. Do we walk in love? Are we imitators of Jesus Christ? Are our reactions to the disabled pleasing to him? Or do we dishonor him by regarding the retarded as having no right to live among the rest of us in freedom and dignity?

It has become increasingly difficult to operate a private facility for any type of health care, whether it be for the retarded, the elderly, the physically handicapped, or the emotionally disturbed. The cost of such a place can be prohibitive, and therefore it has become necessary in most cases to depend upon government funds. Yet it is important that such facilities not be modeled on the cold institutional designs of the past. We need *homes* where profoundly retarded people can live in dignity and where they can be spiritually nurtured as well as physically cared for.

And in this day when the value of human life is threatened in wholesale ways, some suggest that severely handicapped people may be unworthy of life, that the rights of society preclude the burden of expense for caring for the handicapped. Some argue that it would be "kinder" to release them and their families from their suffering and hardship. This can never be an acceptable solution for Christians. The love of God as seen in Jesus Christ must prevail in our lives if we call ourselves his followers.